VEGAN EVERYTHING

100 Easy Recipes for Any Craving—
from Bagels to Burgers, Tacos to Ramen

NADINE HORN & JÖRG MAYER

THE EXPERIMENT
NEW YORK

VEGAN EVERYTHING: *100 Easy Recipes for Any Craving*

Originally published in Germany as *Vegan Kann Jeder* by NeunZehn Verlag in 2014.
First published in North America in revised form by The Experiment, LLC, in 2019.

The Experiment, LLC
220 East 23rd Street, Suite 600
New York, NY 10010-4658
theexperimentpublishing.com

Library of Congress Cataloging-in-Publication Data

Names: Horn, Nadine, author. | Mayer, Jörg, 1983- author.
Title: Vegan everything : 100 easy recipes for any craving /
Nadine Horn & Jörg Mayer.
Description: New York : The Experiment, 2019. | Includes index.
Identifiers: LCCN 2019025399 (print) | LCCN 2019025400 (ebook) | ISBN 9781615195886 (trade paperback) | ISBN 9781615195893 (ebook)
Subjects: LCSH: Vegan cooking. | LCGFT: Cookbooks.
Classification: LCC TX837 .H6936 2019 (print) | LCC TX837 (ebook) | DDC 641.5/6362--dc23
LC record available at https://lccn.loc.gov/2019025399
LC ebook record available at https://lccn.loc.gov/2019025400

ISBN 978-1-61519-588-6
Ebook ISBN 978-1-61519-589-3

Cover design by Beth Bugler
Cover and author photographs by Nadine Horn and Jörg Mayer

Manufactured in China

First printing October 2019

10 9 8 7 6 5 4 3 2 1

DEAR READERS,

In 2006, after eating a vegetarian diet for many years, we decided to take the big step from vegetarianism to veganism. While we appreciate the positive health aspects of a vegan diet, our reasons to make the switch were purely ethical.

We never could have imagined that, five years later, we'd launch a successful vegan food blog at eat-this.org. Or that our blog would lead to our cookbooks, *VBQ—The Ultimate Vegan Barbecue Cookbook* and *The Ultimate Vegan Breakfast Book*, which have allowed us to share our recipes with all of you. We are still amazed!

On our blog, we stay away from detailing the many advantages of a vegan diet, because others have tackled this subject in far more depth. Instead, we focus on the fun aspects of cooking and the joy of delicious vegan food. Such as how new spices can totally change your cooking game. Or how great it feels to attempt a new recipe and have it turn out just as good as we hoped. Or how terrific it feels to shop, cook, and enjoy food consciously, without causing any animals to suffer.

In this cookbook, we hold fast to our focus on the food, without getting bogged down in listing facts or in-depth discussions. We'd much prefer to show you how both beginner and ambitious home cooks like us (remember, we're not trained chefs!) can prepare sophisticated and appetizing dishes perfect for any occasion.

Vegan Everything has many quick and easy recipes for days when you've had a long, hard slog at work and just want something tasty for dinner. It also has more complex recipes for weekends or special occasions, when you've got the time to cook up a big feast for family and friends.

This is our cooking motto: "Vegan, delectable and suitable for daily life." We hope you agree!

Nadine & Jörg

CONTENTS

INFO, TIPS & TRICKS

HOW TO SHOP

RECIPES

HEALTHY START

SNACKS & ON-THE-GO

QUICK MEALS

WONDER BOWLS

COOKING FOR FRIENDS & FAMILY

INFO, TIPS & TRICKS

RECIPE NOTES

We assume that you'll only be using vegan ingredients for our recipes.

Instead of using calorie counts, we've classified our recipes into three categories: "light," "balanced," and "comfort food," each marked with one of the following buttons:

LIGHT BALANCED COMFORT FOOD

Recipes using oats or soy sauce may be labeled "gluten-free." We assume that celiacs or people forgoing gluten will be using the gluten-free versions of these ingredients.

Recipes labeled "sugar-free" means they are free of refined sugar.

Many vegan recipes contain soy, so we've labeled recipes without soy with the label "soy-free."

VEGANISM ISN'T EXPENSIVE

Basic vegan ingredients, which are the building blocks of a vegan diet, are actually quite economical. Vegan alternatives to cheese, yogurt, and meat can cost a bit more, but the bulk of our recipes don't use them in large quantities.

SHOP SMART

When you're looking for fresh produce or spices, the supermarket may not be the cheapest place to shop. For a wide selection and better prices, we recommend always checking farmers markets, specialty grocery stores, and organic supermarkets first.

SHOP IN BULK

We like to buy dry goods like legumes and rice in bulk quantities, which are often cheaper. We then put smaller amounts in glass storage jars to make them easy to access in a busy kitchen.

SHOP SEASONALLY

Buy local produce when it's in season. You'll get the highest quality food at an affordable price. Find out if there's a farm near you; often, buying directly from the source is worth the excursion. You can also look into community-supported agriculture (CSA), which are subscriptions to seasonal produce from local farms, and local farmers markets.

PLAN WELL!

Shopping takes time. If you've planned your meals ahead, you may be able to cut your shopping time down to only once a week. Setting a monthly budget will help you keep your shopping expenses in check.

What you should have with you when you shop:

- A shopping list organized by supermarket aisle
- Your own grocery bags. Plastic bags are bad for the environment and in some cities might even cost you money. In some stores, you may be able to get a small discount for bringing your own bags.

USEFUL EQUIPMENT

Your home kitchen doesn't need to be outfitted with professional-grade equipment to make amazing food. But a few well-selected products will save you money in the long run and can last a lifetime. We recommend two small saucepans, two medium saucepans, one large high-quality pot, a good nonstick pan, and a cast-iron pan. See the section on kitchen tools for a list of our favorites.

Also, avoid buying a slew of cheap knives. We recommend investing in three high-quality knives: a chef's knife, a small paring knife, and a large serrated knife.

MIX 'N' MATCH

Many of the recipes in *Vegan Everything* pair beautifully with our recipes for breads, dips, and sauces. Our favorite combinations can be found in the Tip boxes on the recipe pages.

EAT YOUR LEFTOVERS

Don't throw away your leftovers! They can always be put to good use, repurposed in a stew, or used as a wrap filling to take to work the next day. And whatever can't be reused right away can be stashed in the freezer. Just remember to label it with the contents and the date you made it.

GROW YOUR OWN

Even if you only have a balcony or window sill, you can still put it to good use to grow herbs and maybe even vegetables. Parsley, mint, and basil do well in balcony planters, and chile peppers are very easy to grow from seed in small spaces.

HOW TO SHOP

Cookie

FOR THE FRIDGE

FRESH STUFF

Seasonal produce
Check out your local farmers market and specialty grocery stores in your neighborhood. They are great places to discover new and interesting fruits and vegetables.

Fresh herbs
Parsley, basil, cilantro, and mint can elevate any dish. These herbs will stay fresh longer in the refrigerator when wrapped in damp paper towels.

Ginger, chiles & garlic
Always in our kitchen. They are essential ingredients in many of our recipes.

SEASONINGS

Mustard
Smooth and whole-grain.

Ketchup
We don't only use ketchup in dips and on burgers but also to season sauces and salad dressings.

Sriracha & sambal oelek
Sriracha is an absolute MUST! Spicy and savory, it's not just for stir-fries anymore. We also love sambal oelek (Indonesian chili paste).

Soy sauce
Always in our pantry—it's a very versatile ingredient.

Tomato paste
The perfect savory base for many sauces, soups, and stews.

SUBSTITUTE PRODUCTS

Tofu, seitan & tempeh
Versatile and healthy sources of protein, to make your cooking "meatier."

Soy, oat, rice & almond milks
We like the unsweetened versions of these plant-based milks. They are healthy alternatives to dairy milk for savory recipes.

Coconut or oat cream
Can be used in savory cooking or whipped for sweet desserts.

Vegan butter
Who needs dairy?

FOR THE FREEZER

Frozen vegetables
We always have frozen peas, spinach, and broccoli in our freezer. They're economical, practical, and no less nutritious than their fresh counterparts.

Herbs
We recommend buying fresh herbs in larger quantities. Once washed and dried, extras can be frozen as whole sprigs, such as rosemary or dill, or chopped and frozen with a little water, such as mint and parsley. That way you always have them on hand.

Coconut milk
Freezes nicely, which is convenient if you don't use the whole can. We recommend using full-fat coconut milk for all recipes.

Makrut lime leaves
Impart a wonderful citrusy flavor and aroma. Buy a bag at your local Indian or Asian grocery store—the leaves can be frozen for months.

Breads & doughs
Tortillas and wraps can easily be frozen and are quickly thawed in a pan or the oven. Once yeasted dough has risen, it's also easily frozen. When you're ready to use it, just let it thaw completely and rise again before baking.

Frozen fruit
Frozen berries are perfect for quick smoothies, breakfast cereals, cakes, and muffins.

BOCKSHORNKLEE
MAYO

FOR THE PANTRY

GRAIN PRODUCTS

We often buy rice, noodles, and grains in bulk. Stored in glass or plastic containers, they keep well and are economical to boot.

Rice

We urge you to experiment with different rice varieties. We always have basmati, brown, sushi, and short-grain in our pantry. A well-stocked organic grocery store should have the widest assortment.

Instant couscous

A wonderful side dish when you're pressed for time. Just cover the couscous with boiling water, let swell for five minutes, and it's ready to eat.

Bulgur, polenta & farro

These grains make excellent bases for dishes and are great to have on hand.

Flours

We love experimenting with different types of flour. In this book, you'll find recipes that include buckwheat, chickpea, oat, rice, spelt, and teff flours.

Noodles & pasta

Noodles are a very versatile ingredient in many cuisines. We use traditional wheat pasta, egg-free ramen noodles, glass noodles, rice noodles, and soba.

BEANS & LEGUMES

Dried beans and legumes need to be soaked in water and cooked for a long time (with the exception of lentils). If we're pressed for time, we like to use canned beans, which are already cooked.

SPICES & DRIED HERBS

Spices and herbs are the stars of the kitchen. Be curious and sample your way through your spice rack. We couldn't live without cumin (whole seeds and ground), red pepper flakes, paprika (sweet and smoked), ground allspice, dried oregano, curry powder, garam masala, cinnamon (sticks and ground), fennel seeds, ground sumac, ground turmeric, five-spice powder, and nutmeg.

SWEETENERS

We use conventional sweeteners like granulated, brown, and powdered sugars, but we also use agave and maple syrups, as well as muscovado and unrefined cane sugars in some recipes.

NUTS & SEEDS

Cashews

The most versatile nut. Equally delicious in sweet and savory dishes.

Peanuts & almonds

Provide a delectable crunch in a wide variety of dishes.

Sesame seeds

A particular delight when toasted and served over Asian dishes.

Flaxseed

Ground and mixed with water, it makes a great egg substitute.

OILS

Olive oil

Our go-to oil, which is just as good in a sauté pan as it is in a salad dressing.

Peanut oil

Especially suited for wok-frying tofu, seitan, and vegetables.

Canola oil

A good substitute for olive oil, with a light and nutty flavor. We like to use canola oil when we make our own hot pepper– or garlic-infused oils.

Sesame oil

Dark (toasted) sesame oil should be used very sparingly as a finishing oil.

VINEGARS

Red & white wine vinegar

Rice vinegar

Apple cider vinegar

Balsamic vinegar

THIS & THAT

Vegetable broth

Instant yeast (sometimes called Rapid Rise)

Nutritional yeast

Soy flour

Dried mushrooms (shiitakes, wood ears)

KITCHEN TOOLS

The array of kitchen appliances and specialized gadgets in the kitchen sections of department stores is enormous. But the good news is that you don't actually need most of what's on display! Here is a list of our favorite kitchen tools.

1. CAST-IRON POTS
2. SAUTÉ PANS
3. SHARP KNIVES (CHEF'S KNIFE, SMALL PARING KNIFE, AND LARGE SERRATED KNIFE)
4. CUTTING BOARD
5. FOOD PROCESSOR
6. BLENDER
7. IMMERSION BLENDER
8. GRATER
9. KITCHEN SCALE
10. MEASURING CUPS AND SPOONS
11. SPATULA
12. SKIMMER AND LADLE
13. WHISK
14. ROLLING PIN
15. SIEVE
16. PEELER
17. ELECTRIC KETTLE
18. MORTAR AND PESTLE
19. SMALL BOWLS
20. MIXING BOWLS
21. MUFFIN PAN
22. SPRINGFORM PAN
23. PASTRY BRUSH
24. DISH TOWELS

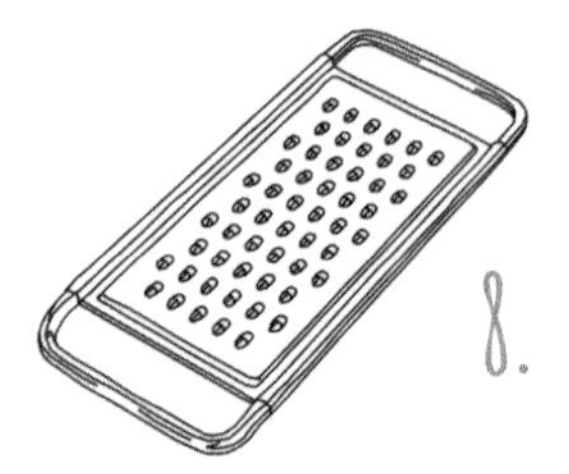

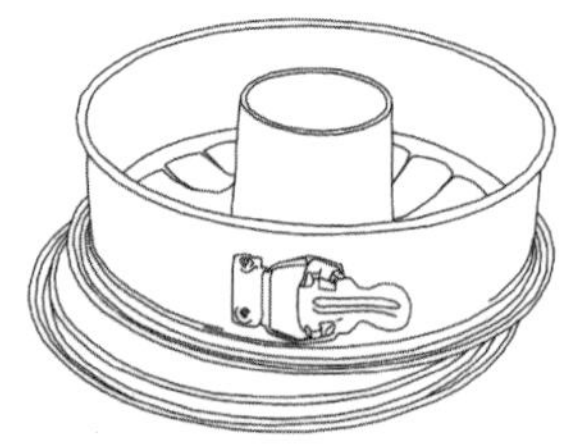

19.
2.
3.
4.
16.
14.
5.
9.
21.
13.
7.
11.
15.
12.
20.
1.
6.
24.

RECIPES

HEALTHY START

MORNING GLORY

COUSCOUS, FRUIT & YOGURT

LIGHT

PREPARATION TIME 10 minutes • SERVES 2

Having a balanced breakfast is a great way to start the day. Here's an excellent option, with lots of fresh berries and fruit, soy yogurt, and carbs.

- ¼ cup (50 g) instant couscous
- 1 small banana
- ¼ cup (60 g) plain soy yogurt
- 2 teaspoons almond butter
- ¼ cup (25 g) fresh or frozen berries
- Handful of grapes
- Pinch of ground cinnamon

1. Bring ⅓ cup (80 ml) water to a boil in a small pot. Add the couscous, cover, and remove from the heat. Let sit for 5 minutes, then uncover and fluff with a fork.
2. Mash the banana with a fork.
3. Layer the couscous, yogurt, banana, almond butter, berries, and grapes in two small glasses or jars until the glasses are filled to the top.
4. Dust with cinnamon.

In summertime, buy or pick as many fresh berries as you can, then freeze them. You can enjoy their sweet flavor all year long!

Enjoy!

SAVORY LOADED WAFFLES

WITH TOFU & AVOCADO

PREPARATION 15 minutes • COOKING TIME About 1 hour • MAKES 8 waffles

Let these delicious waffles with tofu and avocado transport you to the beach for a relaxing breakfast with a California vibe.

FOR THE WAFFLE BATTER

- 2 cups (250 g) all-purpose flour
- 1 tablespoon baking powder
- 2 tablespoons ground flaxseed
- 1 teaspoon onion powder
- 1 teaspoon garlic powder
- 1½ tablespoons olive oil
- ⅔ cup (100 g) drained canned corn kernels
- ½ teaspoon salt

FOR THE TOPPINGS

- 3½ ounces (100 g) smoked tofu
- 1 tablespoon olive oil
- 1 ripe avocado
- 1 scallion
- ¼ cup (60 g) plain soy yogurt
- 2 teaspoons Tabasco sauce
- Juice of ½ lemon

1. Preheat the oven to 200°F (95°C). Preheat the waffle iron to medium-high.
2. To make the waffles, place the flour, baking powder, flaxseed, onion and garlic powders, olive oil, corn, and salt in a bowl with 1½ cups (360 ml) water. Mix until smooth.
3. Pour the batter into the waffle iron, close, and cook until golden brown, 7 to 8 minutes for each waffle. Put the waffle on a baking sheet and keep warm in the oven. Repeat until the batter is gone.
4. While the waffles are cooking, prepare the toppings. Slice the tofu into strips. Heat the oil in a saucepan over high heat. Add the tofu and sauté until crisp and golden brown, about 3 minutes.
5. Pit and peel the avocado. Thinly slice the avocado and scallion.
6. To serve, top each waffle with tofu, avocado, yogurt, scallions, and Tabasco. Drizzle with lemon juice.

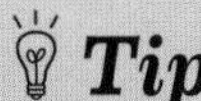

For gluten-free waffles, use the batter from our Savory Corn Waffles (page 149).

Good Morning!

COCONUT FARRO
WITH CARDAMOM & RASPBERRIES

PREPARATION TIME 5 minutes • COOKING TIME 20 minutes • SERVES 2

Farro, a nutritious ancient grain, is packed with protein and minerals. Wonderful in savory dishes, it's also great in this sweet breakfast bowl.

- 3/4 cup (125 g) quick-cooking farro
- 1 cup (240 ml) full-fat coconut milk
- 1/2 teaspoon ground cardamom
- 1/2 teaspoon ground cinnamon
- 2 teaspoons maple syrup
- Generous 1/3 cup (50 g) fresh or frozen raspberries

SOY FREE

1. Place the farro, coconut milk, cardamom, and cinnamon in a small pot over medium heat. Bring to a boil, reduce the heat to low, and simmer for 15 minutes, stirring occasionally, until the farro is tender and the coconut milk is absorbed.

2. Transfer to two bowls, top with the maple syrup and raspberries, and serve.

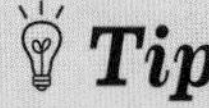

Replace the spices with a bag of chai tea for a delicious Indian-inspired flavor. Simply add the tea bag to the coconut milk when the farro is simmering. Remove before serving!

FRENCH TOAST
WITH MAPLE SYRUP & FRESH FRUIT

PREPARATION TIME 10 minutes • COOKING TIME About 10 minutes • SERVES 2 or 3

A breakfast classic! Wonderfully decadent, French toast is perfect for cozy weekends.

- ½ cup plus 1 tablespoon (135 ml) almond or oat milk
- 2 tablespoons oat flour
- 1 tablespoon rolled oats
- 1 teaspoon ground cinnamon
- Pinch of salt
- 6 slices white bread
- 1 tablespoon coconut oil
- 2 teaspoons maple syrup
- Fresh fruit, optional

1. Combine the milk, oat flour, oats, cinnamon, and salt in a medium bowl.
2. One at a time, soak the bread slices in the liquid mixture for about 20 seconds on each side. Set aside.
3. Heat a large sauté pan over medium heat and melt the coconut oil. Add the bread slices, making sure not to crowd the pan, and cook until golden brown, about 3 minutes on each side. Repeat until all slices have been cooked.
4. Serve with maple syrup and fresh fruit, if desired.

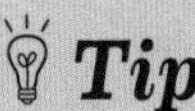

For savory French toast, use olive oil instead of coconut oil and omit the cinnamon. Instead of maple syrup, top with sautéed king oyster mushrooms.

OVERNIGHT OATS

WITH CHIA SEEDS

PREPARATION TIME 10 minutes • SOAKING TIME 4 hours or overnight • SERVES 2

With just a little bit of effort the evening before, you can wake up to a wonderfully creamy breakfast. If you like to take breakfast to work, wait until you get there to combine the oat mixture with the chopped almonds and sliced banana for the best texture.

- 1 cup (100 g) rolled oats
- 1 tablespoon chia seeds
- 2 cups (240 ml) almond milk
- 8 raw almonds
- 1 banana
- 2 teaspoons maple syrup

1. Combine the oats, chia seeds, and almond milk in a medium bowl. Cover and refrigerate for at least 4 hours or overnight.
2. The next morning, toast the almonds in a small pan over medium-high heat, stirring constantly, until fragrant. Let cool briefly, then chop.
3. Slice the banana.
4. Divide the oats between two bowls. Top with the banana, almonds, and maple syrup.

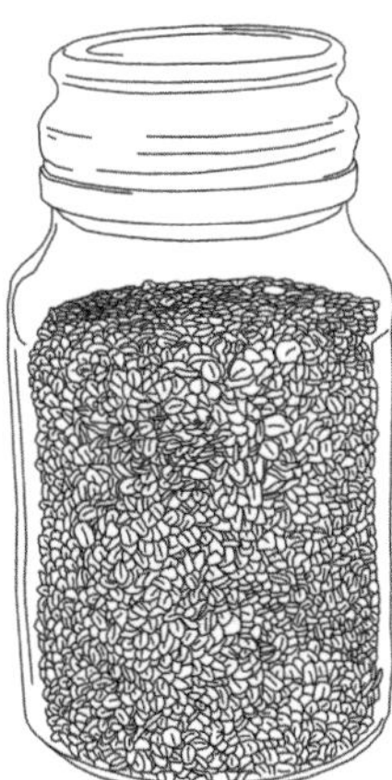

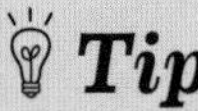

Tip

Oats contain no gluten but are often processed in facilities that also process gluten-containing ingredients. If you are allergic to gluten, be sure to purchase oats that have been processed in a gluten-free facility.

GOOD MOOOOORNING!
GET YOUR ENERGY!

BREAKFAST ENERGY BARS

WITH CRANBERRIES & PECANS

PREPARATION TIME 10 minutes • CHILLING TIME 1 hour • MAKES 10–12 bars

Leave the sweet muffins for dessert and start your day with these healthy homemade energy bars instead. They'll give you the right kind of energy boost.

- 1½ cups (150 g) rolled oats
- ½ cup (80 g) chopped raw almonds
- ½ cup (50 g) chopped pecans
- ¾ cup (100 g) dried cranberries
- 1 cup (50 g) dried coconut chips
- ⅓ cup (80 g) chopped pitted dates
- 2½ tablespoons ground flaxseed
- 2 tablespoons unsweetened applesauce
- 1½ tablespoons maple syrup
- ½ cup (120 g) almond butter
- 1 teaspoon lemon juice
- Pinch of salt

1. Line a 9-inch (23 cm) square baking pan with parchment paper.
2. Combine the oats, almonds, pecans, cranberries, coconut chips, dates, and flaxseed in a large bowl. Add the applesauce and maple syrup and mix well.
3. Whisk together the almond butter, lemon juice, and salt in a small bowl. Add to the oat mixture and mix well. Spoon the mixture into the prepared pan. Use a spatula to smooth it into an even layer.
4. Refrigerate for at least 1 hour.
5. Using a sharp knife, cut into 10 to 12 equal-sized bars.
6. Stored in an airtight container in the fridge, the bars will keep well for at least a week.

Tip

Feel free to swap out the nuts and fruits for ones you have on hand. Dried blueberries, pineapple, apricots, and pistachios all work really well.

SCALLION PANCAKES
WITH TOMATO MACADAMIA RICOTTA

PREPARATION TIME 15 minutes • COOKING TIME About 20 minutes • MAKES 8 pancakes

These pancakes are the perfect hearty breakfast. Their nutty flavor pairs perfectly with our creamy Tomato Macadamia Ricotta.

- 2 scallions
- 2 cups (250 g) buckwheat flour
- 1 teaspoon baking powder
- 1 teaspoon baking soda
- ½ teaspoon salt
- ½ teaspoon freshly ground black pepper
- 2 tablespoons canola oil
- ½ cup (115 g) Tomato Macadamia Ricotta (page 191), for serving

1. Thinly slice the scallions.
2. Whisk the flour, baking powder, baking soda, salt, and pepper with 2 cups (480 ml) water in a medium bowl until smooth. Fold in the scallions.
3. Heat the oil in a large sauté pan over medium-high heat. Working in batches, pour ½ cup (120 ml) of the batter in the pan for each pancake and cook until golden brown, about 4 minutes on each side. Repeat until the batter is gone.
4. Serve with the ricotta.

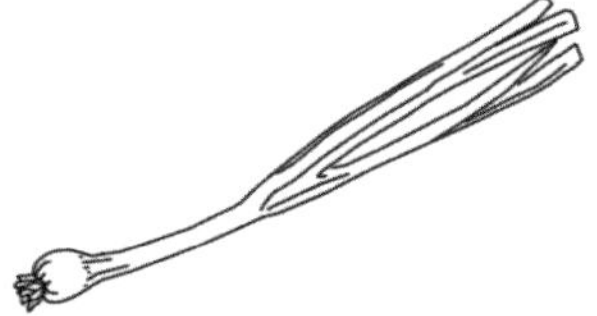

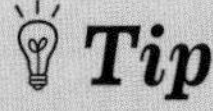

Tip

If you don't like the distinctive flavor of buckwheat, feel free to replace it with wheat, rye, or spelt flour, or fine cornmeal.

YUMMY SMOOTHIES

PREPARATION 5 minutes • SERVES 2

LIGHT

Shake up your smoothie routine!
Here are some lovely alternatives to the green standard.

GREEN HORNET

1 banana, peeled

2 kiwis, peeled and diced

4 stalks curly kale, stemmed

3 tablespoons fresh parsley

1 teaspoon wheat grass powder

1¼ cups (300 ml) water

4 ice cubes

WAKE UP

2 carrots, peeled

½ ripe mango, peeled and cubed

1 thumb-sized piece fresh ginger, peeled and grated

¾ cup (180 ml) freshly squeezed orange juice

½ cup (120 ml) apple juice

4 ice cubes

BANANA JOE

2 bananas, peeled

Handful of rolled oats

1¼ cups (300 ml) almond milk

5 raw almonds

Pinch of ground cinnamon

4 ice cubes

CHUCK BERRY

3 tablespoons fresh or frozen berries

5 raw almonds

1¼ cups (300 ml) almond milk

4 ice cubes

Combine the ingredients in a high-speed blender and blend until smooth. Serve immediately.

SNACKS & ON-THE-GO

BÁNH MÌ DELUXE

WITH PICKLES & MOCK DUCK

PREPARATION TIME 20 minutes • COOKING TIME 10 minutes • SERVES 4

A classic Vietnamese street food, bánh mì sandwiches are now popular all over the world. We love the combination of crisp French bread with traditional Southeast Asian flavors.

- 9 ounces (250 g) mock duck or seitan
- 2 tablespoons peanut oil
- ½ cucumber
- 2 garlic cloves
- 2 teaspoons sesame oil
- 4 bánh mì or other bread rolls
- 4 tablespoons Basic or Sriracha Mayo (page 183)
- ½ cup (80 g) drained Vietnamese Pickles (page 189)
- ½ bunch fresh cilantro

1. Cut or tear the mock duck into bite-sized pieces.
2. Heat the peanut oil in a sauté pan over medium-high heat. Add the mock duck and sauté, turning occasionally, for about 8 minutes, until crisp. Set aside in a medium bowl.
3. Thinly slice the cucumber into strips 1½ inches (4 cm) long.
4. Mince the garlic and add to the fried mock duck along with the sesame oil. Mix.
5. Slice the rolls in half and spread with the mayo. Layer the mock duck, cucumber, pickles, and cilantro on the bread, then close the sandwiches. Serve immediately.

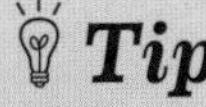

Tip

Mock duck is a versatile flavored seitan that is delicious in many different Asian recipes. Find it at vegetarian grocery stores or online.

VIETNAMESE CUCUMBER SALAD

WITH CILANTRO & ROASTED PEANUTS

PREPARATION TIME 15 minutes • SERVES 4

This fresh and spicy summer salad topped with crunchy roasted peanuts is perfect for your next vegan barbecue or as a side dish to your favorite Asian stir-fry.

- 1 medium cucumber
- 1 tablespoon unsalted raw peanuts
- 1 teaspoon sesame seeds
- 2 scallions
- 1 fresh Thai red chile
- 1 garlic clove
- 3 tablespoons rice vinegar
- 1 tablespoon agave syrup
- 1 tablespoon chopped fresh mint
- 1 tablespoon chopped fresh cilantro

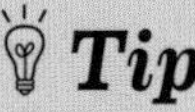

1. Slice the cucumber in half lengthwise. Remove the seeds with a spoon. Cut the cucumber into half-moons ½ inch (13 mm) thick and arrange on a serving plate.
2. Toast the peanuts and sesame seeds in a dry pan over medium-high heat for 4 minutes, stirring constantly, until golden brown. Set aside to cool.
3. Thinly slice the scallions, chile, and garlic. Distribute them evenly over the cucumber.
4. For the dressing, whisk together the vinegar and agave syrup. Pour over the salad and toss to coat.
5. Top with the mint and cilantro and the toasted seeds and nuts.

Tip

We love mixing up this salad with fresh radishes and cherry tomatoes, as well as using fresh lime juice instead of rice vinegar.

WE LOVE KALE!

SAVORY KALE CHIPS

OUR HEALTHY TV SNACK

SOAKING TIME 8 hours or overnight • PREPARATION TIME 10 minutes
BAKING TIME 1 hour • SERVES 4

Kale is a very versatile ingredient. Try it in smoothies, stir-fries, and stews or as a healthy snack!

- ⅔ cup (100 g) raw cashews
- 1 bunch curly kale
- 3 tablespoons nutritional yeast
- 1 garlic clove
- 1 teaspoon ground paprika
- 1 teaspoon salt
- 1 tablespoon liquid smoke
- 1 tablespoon lemon juice

1. Soak the cashews in a bowl of water for at least 8 hours or overnight.
2. Preheat the oven to 200°F (95°C). Line two baking sheets with parchment paper.
3. Strip the kale leaves from the stems and discard the stems. Tear the leaves into bite-sized pieces and place in a medium bowl.
4. Drain the cashews. Combine the cashews, nutritional yeast, garlic, paprika, salt, liquid smoke, and lemon juice in a high-speed blender with ⅓ cup (75 ml) water and blend until smooth.
5. Pour the blended cashews over the kale and mix well.
6. Divide the kale evenly between the baking sheets, spreading it in an even layer. Bake until crisp, about 1 hour, turning the kale leaves after 30 minutes.
7. Let cool and store in an airtight container.

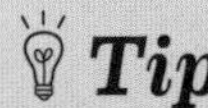

Tip

A few drops of liquid smoke gives the kale chips a savory, smoky flavor.

LONDON SANDWICHES

WITH HUMMUS & FRESH SPROUTS

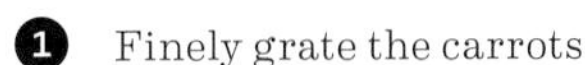

PREPARATION TIME 10 minutes • SERVES 4

We first discovered this yummy sandwich while traveling in London. Now we can't imagine our lives without it. We like it as a snack between meals, as a light dinner, or when we're on the go.

- 2 carrots, peeled
- One 15-ounce (425 g) can chickpeas, drained
- 1½ tablespoons tahini
- Juice of ½ lemon
- 1 garlic clove, minced
- Salt and freshly ground black pepper
- 8 slices whole wheat sandwich bread
- 1 cup (100 g) fresh bean sprouts (see Tip)
- 4 lettuce leaves

1. Finely grate the carrots.
2. Combine the chickpeas, tahini, lemon juice, and garlic in a food processor and pulse until smooth. Season the hummus to taste with salt and pepper.
3. Toast the bread.
4. Spread the hummus generously on the bread. Top four of the slices with grated carrots, sprouts, and lettuce leaves, then top with the remaining bread.

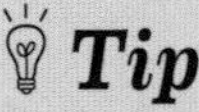

Tip

Raw bean sprouts carry a risk of foodborne illness and as a result can be hard to find in stores. If you cannot find sprouts in your local market, we suggest using shredded cucumber as a substitute.

CHICKPEA SUMAC SALAD

BRING ON SUMMER!

PREPARATION TIME 25 minutes • CHILLING TIME 30 minutes • SERVES 4

Sumac, available in well-stocked grocery stores and Middle Eastern markets, is popular in countries such as Turkey and Iran. Made from finely ground sumac berries, this tart spice is essential to many different Middle Eastern–inspired dishes. We love using it to add a zing to salads.

- 1 red onion
- 1 teaspoon salt
- 2 tablespoons ground sumac
- 1 teaspoon ground cayenne
- ¼ Preserved Lemon (page 185)
- 2 garlic cloves
- ½ bunch fresh parsley
- Handful of cherry tomatoes
- Two 15-ounce (425 g) cans chickpeas, drained
- ¼ cup (60 ml) olive oil
- 2 tablespoons pomegranate molasses
- Salt and freshly ground black pepper

1. Slice the onion into thin rings. Combine the onion with the salt, sumac, and cayenne in a large bowl, mixing well.
2. Slice the lemon into thin strips. Mince the garlic and parsley. Halve the tomatoes.
3. Add the garlic, parsley, and tomatoes to the onions, then fold in the chickpeas and lemon.
4. Drizzle the salad with the oil and pomegranate molasses. Season to taste with salt and pepper and toss to coat.

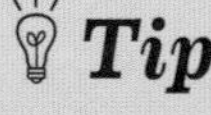

Tip

If you don't have preserved lemons in your pantry, you can use the juice of half a lemon instead. Serve the salad with Savory Scones (page 171) or Flatbread (page 169).

DRIED ROSEMARY
&
GOOD OLIVE OIL

ROSEMARY CRACKERS

A TASTE OF ITALY IN YOUR HOME

PREPARATION TIME 10 minutes • BAKING TIME 15 minutes • MAKES 12 to 16 crackers

These golden-brown crackers, infused with the delicious Mediterranean flavors of rosemary and olive oil, are great as a snack or appetizer.

- 1¾ cups (200 g) spelt flour
- ¼ cup (15 g) dried rosemary
- 2 teaspoons salt
- 1 teaspoon freshly ground black pepper
- ¼ cup plus 2 tablespoons (90 ml) olive oil

1. Preheat the oven to 325°F (165°C). Line a baking sheet with parchment paper.
2. Mix the flour, rosemary, salt, pepper, and oil in a medium bowl. Gradually add a scant ½ cup (100 ml) water, stirring constantly. When all the water has been added, use your hands to knead the dough until smooth.
3. Take the parchment paper off the baking sheet and place it on your work surface. Roll out the dough on the paper so that it fits perfectly. Place the paper with the dough back on the baking sheet. Using a knife, score the dough to make 12 to 16 crackers, but do not cut all the way through.
4. Bake for 15 minutes, or until golden brown. Let the crackers cool on the baking sheet on a wire rack. The crackers will crisp as they cool. Break into pieces to serve.

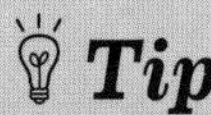

Tip

This is a great party snack! Serve with olives, one of our delicious dips (pages 181 and 191) or Aged Cashew Cheese (page 193) along with a glass of good vegan red wine.

CALIFORNIA RICE SALAD

WITH TOFU, GRAPES & ALMONDS

PREPARATION TIME 20 minutes • COOKING TIME 40 minutes • SERVES 4

Crisp fried tofu meets sweet grapes and nutty roasted almonds—a wonderful late summer lunch or dinner.

- 1⅔ cups (300 g) brown rice
- 7 ounces (200 g) firm tofu
- 1 tablespoon cornstarch
- 2 tablespoons peanut oil
- 2 tablespoons raw almonds
- ⅓ cup (50 g) grapes
- 1 tablespoon drained capers
- ¼ cup plus 2 tablespoons (90 g) Basic Mayo (page 183)
- 2 tablespoons apple cider vinegar
- Salt and freshly ground black pepper

1. Combine the rice and 2½ cups (600 ml) water in a medium pot. Bring to a boil, reduce the heat to low, and cover. Cook for 30 minutes, undisturbed. Turn off the heat and let stand for 10 minutes, then fluff with a fork.
2. While the rice cooks, cut the tofu into 1½-inch (4 cm) cubes and dredge in the cornstarch.
3. Heat the oil in a sauté pan over medium-high heat. Sauté the tofu until crisp on all sides, about 8 minutes.
4. Toast the almonds in a dry pan over medium-high heat for about 4 minutes, stirring constantly, until golden brown. Let cool, then chop coarsely.
5. Halve the grapes.
6. Place the rice in a large serving bowl. Break up the tofu cubes and fold into the rice. Mix in the grapes, capers, almonds, mayo, and vinegar. Season to taste with salt and pepper.

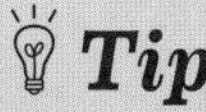

A cold dry white wine or beer is a great accompaniment to this salad. The salad travels nicely to work (but maybe leave the beer or wine at home).

SNACK ATTACK!

ROASTED CHICKPEAS

A CRUNCHY SNACK FOR BETWEEN MEALS

PREPARATION TIME 5 minutes • BAKING TIME 30 minutes • SERVES 4

Are you craving a healthy, savory snack?
These crisp chickpeas are just the ticket.

One 15-ounce (425 g) can chickpeas

1 tablespoon olive oil

½ teaspoon coarse sea salt

½ teaspoon ground cumin

½ teaspoon ground fennel seeds

½ teaspoon ground coriander

½ teaspoon ground paprika

1. Preheat the oven to 325°F (165°C). Line a rimmed baking sheet with parchment paper.
2. Drain and dry the chickpeas completely with a dish towel or paper towels. Put in a medium bowl, add the oil, salt, cumin, fennel, coriander, and paprika and mix well.
3. Spread the chickpeas out evenly onto the baking sheet. Roast for 30 minutes, or until crisp and golden brown. Serve hot or cold. Store in an airtight container.

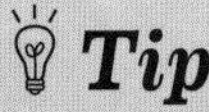

Tip

Try making these chickpeas with your favorite spices or seasoning blends. This recipe also works well with other beans, such as kidney or white beans.

QUICK MEALS

Fennel
+ Lemon
= delicious

SAUTÉED FENNEL

WITH COUSCOUS & LEMON

PREPARATION TIME 20 minutes • SERVES 4

Fennel, with its delicate anise flavor, is rich in vitamin C and calcium. Fresh fennel should be bright green, with no brown marks on its outer layers. Otherwise it will turn dry and woody when cooked.

- 1 cup (200 g) instant couscous
- 2 fennel bulbs (1 pound/450 g each)
- 5 tablespoons olive oil
- 1 cup (200 g) cooked white beans
- Juice of 1 lemon
- Salt and freshly ground black pepper
- ½ bunch fresh parsley, finely chopped

1. Bring 1½ cups (360 ml) water to a boil in a small pot. Add the couscous, cover, and remove from the heat. Let sit for 5 minutes, then uncover and fluff with a fork.
2. Trim the stalks from the fennel. Chop the fennel fronds and set aside. Quarter the bulbs and cut out the cores. Cut into slices ½ inch (13 mm) thick.
3. Heat 2 tablespoons of the oil in a sauté pan over medium-high heat. Add the sliced fennel and cook for about 8 minutes, turning over the slices after 4 minutes, until golden brown.
4. Remove from the heat. Mix in the beans and let sit in the warm pan for about 3 minutes.
5. Transfer the couscous to a serving bowl and top with the fennel and beans. Drizzle with the lemon juice and the remaining 3 tablespoons oil.
6. Season with salt and pepper to taste. Garnish with the reserved fennel fronds and the parsley.

Tip

Thinly sliced or grated, raw fennel is delicious. We also like it in a Middle Eastern–inspired salad with lentils.

Super easy & super delicious!

ALOO TIKKA

WITH CUCUMBER-MINT RAITA

PREPARATION TIME 20 minutes • COOKING TIME About 15 minutes • MAKES 12 patties

These Indian potato patties are terrific finger food. Rolled up in crunchy lettuce leaves and topped with cooling raita, they will disappear like magic.

FOR THE CUCUMBER-MINT RAITA

¼ medium cucumber, peeled and seeded

½ bunch fresh mint, leaves only

1⅓ cups (300 g) plain soy yogurt

½ teaspoon salt

FOR THE ALOO TIKKA

1 pound (500 g) russet potatoes, boiled until soft

1 medium red onion

½ cup (50 g) bread crumbs

1 jalapeño, chopped

1 teaspoon ground coriander

½ teaspoon ground cumin

1 teaspoon salt

¼ cup (60 ml) canola oil

FOR SERVING

12 large romaine lettuce leaves

1. To make the the raita, dice the cucumber and chop the mint. Combine them with the yogurt, mixing well. Season with the salt. Refrigerate until serving.
2. To make the tikka, peel the potatoes and cut into chunks. Mince the onion.
3. Place the potatoes, bread crumbs, jalapeño, coriander, cumin, and salt in a food processor and pulse until smooth. Fold in the onion.
4. With wet hands, form into 12 patties.
5. Heat the oil in a sauté pan over medium-high heat. Working in batches if necessary, fry the patties until golden brown, about 4 minutes on each side. Drain on paper towels.
6. Place each patty on a lettuce leaf and serve topped with raita.

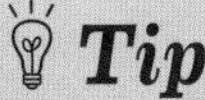

Tip

You can vary the flavor of the aloo tikka by adding peas, grated fresh ginger, or different Indian spices.

AFRICAN PEANUT STEW

WITH BEANS & PEANUTS

PREPARATION TIME 10 minutes • COOKING TIME 20 minutes • SERVES 4

This is one of our go-to recipes when we're pressed for time. It might not look like much, but the flavor is phenomenal, it's incredibly filling, and it's easy to prepare! Serve with rice, couscous, or millet.

- 2 onions
- 3 garlic cloves
- 2 tablespoons peanut oil
- 6 medium Roma tomatoes
- One 15-ounce (425 g) can kidney beans, drained
- 1 tablespoon natural peanut butter
- 2 teaspoons sambal oelek (Indonesian chili paste)
- 1 teaspoon ground cumin
- 1 teaspoon salt
- Cilantro, to serve

1. Finely dice the onions. Thinly slice the garlic.
2. Heat the oil in a saucepan over medium heat. Add the onion and garlic and cook until translucent, about 4 minutes.
3. Cube the tomatoes and add to the pan. Reduce the heat to low and cook for 10 minutes, until the tomatoes soften.
4. Add the beans, peanut butter, sambal, cumin, and salt and simmer for 5 minutes, until hot.
5. Remove from the heat, garnish with cilantro, and serve.

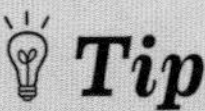

Tip

If you're making this dish when good fresh tomatoes are in short supply, you can substitute a drained 28-ounce (794 g) can diced tomatoes.

FRITTATA

WITH OYSTER MUSHROOMS

PREPARATION TIME 20 minutes • COOKING TIME 40 minutes • SERVES 2

You wouldn't normally associate an Italian egg dish with vegan cuisine. But tofu makes a great egg substitute in this easy, savory plant-based frittata.

- 1 onion
- 9 ounces (250 g) fresh oyster mushrooms
- 3 tablespoons olive oil
- 10½ ounces (300 g) silken tofu
- 3 tablespoons cornstarch
- 2 tablespoons nutritional yeast
- ½ teaspoon ground turmeric
- ½ teaspoon onion powder
- ½ teaspoon garlic powder
- 1 teaspoon salt
- ½ teaspoon freshly ground black pepper
- 5 ounces (150 g) firm tofu
- Parsley, to serve

1. Preheat the oven to 350°F (180°C).
2. Dice the onion and coarsely chop the mushrooms.
3. Heat 1 tablespoon of the oil in an oven-safe sauté pan over medium-high heat. Cook the onion for about 3 minutes, until translucent.
4. Add the mushrooms and cook for 5 minutes, stirring occasionally.
5. While the mushrooms are cooking, purée the silken tofu, cornstarch, nutritional yeast, turmeric, onion and garlic powders, salt, pepper, and the remaining 2 tablespoons oil in a food processor. Crumble the firm tofu and fold into the puréed tofu mixture.
6. Reduce to the heat to medium. Pour the tofu mixture over the mushrooms and cook for 10 minutes, or until the frittata sets.
7. Transfer the pan to the oven and bake for 20 minutes, or until golden brown. Top with parsley, cut into wedges, and serve.

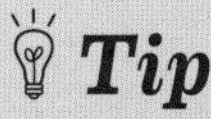

Tip

This frittata is also delicious with asparagus, zucchini strips, or sun-dried tomatoes. Our Dinner Rolls (page 173) and a salad round it out to a wholesome meal.

SESAME NOODLES
WITH CUCUMBERS

PREPARATION TIME 20 minutes • SERVES 4

These cold noodles—with nutty sesame, fresh cucumbers, and a creamy sauce—are the perfect light summer meal.

- 1 pound (500 g) noodles
- 1 tablespoon dark (toasted) sesame oil
- 1 garlic clove
- ½ medium cucumber
- 2 scallions
- 2 teaspoons black sesame seeds
- 3 tablespoons Chinese sesame paste or tahini
- 2 tablespoons natural peanut butter
- 3 tablespoons rice vinegar
- 2 tablespoons soy sauce
- ½ teaspoon salt

1. Bring a large pot of water to a boil. Add the noodles, stirring gently. Lower the heat to a simmer and cook for about 4 minutes, until barely tender.
2. Drain the noodles and transfer to a bowl of cold water to remove excess starch. Drain again and put the noodles in a medium bowl. Dress with ½ teaspoon of the sesame oil and set aside.
3. Mince the garlic, slice the cucumber into 3-inch (7.5 cm) strips, and thinly slice the scallions.
4. Toast the sesame seeds in a dry pan over medium-high heat for about 4 minutes, stirring constantly, until golden brown. Set aside to cool.
5. Combine the garlic, sesame paste, peanut butter, vinegar, the remaining 2 ½ teaspoons sesame oil, and the soy sauce in a small bowl. Mix well, seasoning with the salt.
6. Pour the dressing over the noodles and mix well. Top with the scallions, cucumbers, and sesame seeds.

Tip

For an alternative to Asian noodles, you can also try this recipe with whole wheat spaghetti. For the right texture, cook the pasta a little more than al dente.

CRUNCHY!

SPINACH FALAFEL

WITH MINTED SOY YOGURT

PREPARATION TIME 20 minutes • SOAKING TIME 8 hours • MAKES 16 falafel balls

Finger food doesn't always have to be unhealthy. Our falafel isn't deep-fried but rather panfried in olive oil until crisp. The combination of spinach and chickpeas tastes great and is good for you.

FOR THE FALAFEL

- 1 cup (200 g) dried chickpeas
- ½ onion
- 3 garlic cloves, peeled
- 1½ teaspoons baking powder
- 2 teaspoons ground cumin
- 1 teaspoon salt
- 8 ounces (225 g) fresh spinach, chopped
- ¼ cup plus 2 tablespoons (90 ml) olive oil

FOR THE MINTED SOY YOGURT

- ½ bunch fresh mint
- 1 cup (200 g) plain soy yogurt
- Juice of ½ lemon
- Salt and freshly ground black pepper

1. To make the falafel, place the chickpeas in a large bowl and cover with water. Set aside for 8 hours or overnight.
2. Drain the chickpeas. Dice the onion and garlic. Combine the chickpeas, onion, and garlic in a food processor with the baking powder, cumin, and salt. Pulse until finely chopped but not puréed.
3. Fold the spinach into the chickpea mixture.
4. Wet your hands and roll the mixture into 16 falafel balls, slightly flattened.
5. To make the minted soy yogurt, finely chop the mint. Mix the yogurt, lemon juice, and mint together in a small bowl, then season to taste with salt and pepper. Set aside.
6. Heat the oil in a small saucepan over medium-high heat. Fry the falafel in the hot oil in batches until crisp all over, about 4 minutes per falafel ball. Don't crowd the pan. Remove from the oil and drain on paper towels.
7. Serve the warm falafel with the minted soy yogurt.

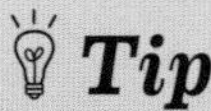

Tip

Wrap the falafel in romaine lettuce leaves or a flexible flatbread for a portable snack.

OSTERIA
AT
HOME

OLIVE RAGÙ

ON HERBED POLENTA

BALANCED

COOKING TIME 25 minutes • SERVES 4

Try our super speedy ragù with hearty black olives, fresh oregano, and ground bay leaf. We like to serve it over a creamy polenta flecked with fresh herbs.

FOR THE HERBED POLENTA

- Salt
- 1¾ cups (300 g) instant polenta
- ½ bunch fresh basil
- 1 teaspoon freshly ground black pepper

FOR THE RAGÙ

- 1⅓ cups (200 g) cured black olives
- 1 carrot, peeled
- 1 stalk celery
- 2 tablespoons olive oil
- 3 tablespoons red wine
- 3 tablespoons fresh oregano leaves
- 1 teaspoon ground fennel seeds
- ¼ teaspoon ground bay leaves
- Basil, to serve

1. To make the polenta, bring 7 cups (1.65 L) salted water to a boil in a large pot. Slowly add the polenta, whisking constantly until there are no lumps. Reduce the heat to low and simmer, whisking until the polenta starts to thicken, about 5 minutes. Let simmer on low heat for 10 more minutes.
2. Pit the olives and finely chop them together with the carrot and celery.
3. Heat the oil in a saucepan over medium-high heat. Add the chopped vegetables and cook for a few minutes, until they begin to soften.
4. Add the wine, oregano, fennel, and bay leaf. Reduce the heat to medium, cover the pot, and simmer for about 6 minutes, until the wine evaporates. Season to taste with salt and pepper.
5. Coarsely chop the basil and fold into the polenta. Mix in the pepper and salt to taste.
6. Spoon the olive ragù over the polenta, top with basil, and serve.

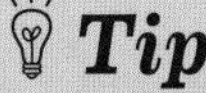

Try the ragù topped with our homemade Vegan Parmesan: Grind ⅔ cup (100 g) raw cashews, 1 cup plus 1 tablespoon (70 g) nutritional yeast, and ¼ teaspoon salt in a food processor.

VEGAN PARMESAN

GREEN POWER WRAPS

PLANT-POWERED STREET FOOD

PREPARATION TIME 10 minutes • COOKING TIME 20 minutes • MAKES 4 wraps

Wrap sandwiches are beloved as street-food snacks all over the world, in all different kinds of variations. For this perfect on-the-go meal, we've combined Mexican tortillas with vegetables cooked with Asian flavors.

- Salt
- ½ head broccoli (about 5 ounces/140 g)
- 1 bunch curly kale
- 1 red jalapeño
- 2 garlic cloves
- 2 scallions
- 7 ounces (200 g) firm tofu
- 2 tablespoons peanut oil
- 3 tablespoons sriracha
- 2 tablespoons soy sauce
- 1 tablespoon rice vinegar
- 1 teaspoon dark (toasted) sesame oil
- 4 large flour tortillas
- ¼ bunch fresh cilantro, chopped

1. Bring a large pot of salted water to a boil. Fill a large bowl with cold water and ice to make an ice bath.
2. Cut the broccoli into florets. Stem and coarsely chop the kale. Blanch the vegetables in the boiling water for 5 minutes.
3. Transfer the vegetables to the ice bath immediately to stop the cooking process. When cool, drain.
4. Finely mince the jalapeño and garlic. Thinly slice the scallions, separating the white and green parts. Cut the tofu into 1½-inch (4 cm) cubes.
5. Heat the peanut oil in a sauté pan over medium-high heat. Add the white parts of the scallion and sauté for a few minutes, until softened. Add the tofu and sauté for 5 minutes, stirring frequently.
6. Reduce the heat to medium. Add the broccoli, kale, jalapeño, garlic, and scallion greens and cook for an additional 5 minutes, stirring frequently, until the vegetables are bright green.
7. Mix in the sriracha, soy sauce, rice vinegar, and sesame oil and remove from the heat.
8. Warm the tortillas in a dry pan over medium-high heat. Top with the vegetables and the cilantro. Roll up and serve.

Tip

Use any kind of wrap large enough to roll into a satisfyingly large sandwich. We highly recommend serving these wraps with our Yum Yum Sauce (page 195).

SHEET-PAN SUPER SUPPER
WITH ROASTED RED PEPPER HUMMUS

PREPARATION TIME 10 minutes • BAKING TIME 30 minutes • SERVES 4

Roasted vegetables can be kind of ho-hum. But this sheet-pan dish, with its exciting seasonings, rich assortment of veggies, and creamy dip, makes for a great dinner.

FOR THE VEGETABLES

14 ounces (400 g) russet potatoes
2 carrots, peeled
2 parsnips, peeled
4 shallots
1 cup (100 g) brussels sprouts
¼ cup (60 ml) olive oil
1 teaspoon dried rosemary
1 teaspoon ground paprika
½ teaspoon dried thyme
½ teaspoon dried oregano
1 teaspoon salt
½ teaspoon freshly ground black pepper

FOR THE HUMMUS

2 roasted red bell peppers, stemmed and seeded
One 15-ounce (425 g) can chickpeas, drained
1 tablespoon nutritional yeast
2 teaspoons tomato paste
1 garlic clove
1 teaspoon agave syrup
½ teaspoon salt

1. Preheat the oven to 400°F (200°C). Line a baking sheet with parchment paper.

2. To roast the vegetables, quarter the potatoes. Cut the carrots and parsnips into long strips. Halve the shallots and brussels sprouts.

3. Put the vegetables in a bowl and mix with the oil, rosemary, paprika, thyme, oregano, salt, and pepper. Spread out in an even layer on the prepared baking sheet and roast for 30 minutes, stirring once after 15 minutes, until cooked through and browned.

4. While the vegetables are roasting, make the hummus. Place the roasted peppers, chickpeas, nutritional yeast, tomato paste, garlic, agave syrup, and salt in a food processor and purée until smooth. Transfer to a bowl and serve with the roasted vegetables.

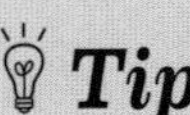
Tip

Potatoes or sweet potatoes should always form the base of this sheet-pan meal, but you can substitute any vegetable you love for the other vegetables.

SPEEDY RAMEN

JAPANESE NOODLE SOUP

PREPARATION TIME 20 minutes • COOKING 10 minutes • SERVES 4

Homemade ramen soup is totally different from the highly processed packages you find in any corner store. No synthetic flavor enhancers for us! We pack our ramen broth full of fresh vegetables, miso, and tofu.

- 2 quarts (2 L) vegetable broth
- 1 tablespoon soy sauce
- 2 teaspoons dark (toasted) sesame oil
- 10½ ounces (300 g) egg-free ramen noodles
- 2 carrots, peeled
- 7 ounces (200 g) firm tofu
- 2 scallions
- 1 cup (100 g) fresh bean sprouts
- 2 red jalapeños or other fresh red chiles
- ½ teaspoon pink peppercorns
- ½ teaspoon freshly ground black pepper
- ¼ cup (70 g) yellow miso paste

1. Bring the broth, soy sauce, and sesame oil to a boil in a large pot over high heat.
2. Add the noodles and cook for 4 to 5 minutes, until just tender. Remove the noodles with tongs and divide among four serving bowls, leaving the broth at a boil.
3. Shave the carrot into thin strips. Cut the tofu into ¾-inch (20 mm) cubes. Thinly slice the scallions at an angle.
4. Add the carrot, tofu, scallions, and bean sprouts to the broth and boil for 3 minutes, until softened. Using a slotted spoon, remove them from the pot and divide among the soup bowls.
5. Finely chop the jalapeños and grind the peppercorns. Add them to the broth with the black pepper. Bring to a rapid boil.
6. Remove from the heat and stir in the miso.
7. Divide the broth among the soup bowls and serve immediately.

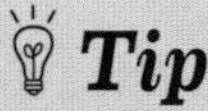

The sky's the limit when it comes to the toppings and mix-ins for this soup. Any kind of steamed or raw vegetable would work, especially thinly sliced mushrooms like enoki, shiitake, or even button mushrooms, as well as tofu in any form.

WONDER BOWLS

SPICY COCONUT SOUP

WITH RICE NOODLES

PREPARATION TIME 10 minutes • COOKING TIME 10 minutes • SERVES 4

You definitely need to try our take on one of Thailand's most famous dishes, a fragrant soup called tom yum, which is full of Southeast Asian flavors and aromas. You can play around with the level of heat to taste.

One 13.5-ounce (400 ml) can full-fat coconut milk

1 cup (240 ml) soy milk

3 makrut lime leaves

¼ cup (60 ml) soy sauce

1 thumb-sized piece ginger

1 garlic clove

1 stalk lemongrass

½ yellow bell pepper, stemmed and seeded

½ green bell pepper, stemmed and seeded

1 large carrot, peeled

3½ ounces (100 g) white button mushrooms

½ cup (75 g) drained canned bamboo shoots

3 ounces (75 g) rice vermicelli

1 tablespoon sambal oelek (Indonesian chili paste)

2 teaspoons dark (toasted) sesame oil

½ bunch fresh cilantro

1. Bring the coconut milk, soy milk, 1 cup (240 ml) water, the lime leaves, and soy sauce to a boil in a saucepan over medium-high heat.
2. Finely mince the ginger and garlic. Crush the lemongrass with the flat side of a knife. Cut the bell peppers and carrot into thin strips. Quarter the mushrooms and thinly slice the bamboo shoots.
3. Add the ginger, garlic, lemongrass, bell peppers, carrot, mushrooms, and bamboo shoots to the broth. Bring to a boil, then reduce the heat to low and simmer for 10 minutes. After 5 minutes, remove the lemongrass and add the rice vermicelli, cooking until just tender.
4. Stir together the sambal oelek and sesame oil in a small bowl. Coarsely chop the cilantro.
5. Divide the soup among four serving bowls. Top with the sauce and cilantro and serve immediately.

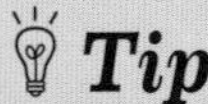

Tip

Feel free to vary the mix-ins. We also love the coconut broth with cubed tofu, water chestnuts, fresh bok choy, baby corn, or tiny Thai eggplant.

RICE NOODLES + SPINACH + SESAME SEEDS

ASIAN RICE NOODLE SALAD

WITH BABY SPINACH

PREPARATION TIME 25 minutes • SERVES 4

Asian rice noodles are a delicious and often gluten-free alternative to durum wheat noodles. They're really versatile and work well in stir-fries and salads, or tossed in a delicious sauce.

7 ounces (200 g) wide rice noodles
2 tablespoons sesame seeds
1 shallot
1 thumb-sized piece ginger
2 garlic cloves
1 red jalapeño or other fresh chile
¼ bunch fresh cilantro
¼ cup (60 ml) soy sauce
3 tablespoons rice vinegar
1 teaspoon dark (toasted) sesame oil
Juice of 1 lemon
2 carrots, peeled
10½ ounces (300 g) baby spinach

1. Cook the noodles according to the package instructions. Drain and rinse under cold running water. Drain again.
2. Toast the sesame seeds in a dry pan over medium-high heat for about 4 minutes, stirring constantly, until golden brown. Set aside.
3. Finely chop the shallot, ginger, garlic, jalapeño, and cilantro. Mix together in a large bowl with the soy sauce, vinegar, oil, and lemon juice to make the dressing.
4. Cut the carrot into thin strips.
5. Toss the spinach, noodles, and carrots with the dressing. Garnish with the toasted sesame seeds and serve immediately.

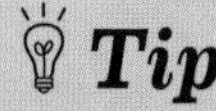

Tip

Rice noodles come in many sizes and cook quickly. Thinner noodles can often be cooked by soaking them in very hot water for a few minutes.

Hot
&
spicy!

FIERY KOSHARI

PREPARATION TIME 10 minutes • COOKING TIME 35 minutes • SERVES 4

Koshari, *one of Egypt's national dishes, is an unusual mix of rice, noodles, and lentils, served with a spicy tomato sauce. Beloved at breakfast, it can be found on every street corner in Cairo.*

1 red onion

3 tablespoons olive oil

1½ tablespoons ground cumin

1 tablespoon coriander seeds

1½ teaspoons red pepper flakes

1 teaspoon ground paprika

½ teaspoon ground allspice

One 14.5-ounce (411 g) can diced tomatoes

1½ cups (150 g) ditalini or other small macaroni

½ cup (100 g) long-grain white rice

⅓ cup (75 g) red lentils

1 red jalapeño or other fresh red chile

2 tablespoons white wine vinegar

Salt and freshly ground black pepper

Tip

Minted Soy Yogurt (page 65) is a nice accompaniment to this spicy koshari. To make a small amount, just season a few tablespoons of plain soy yogurt with a pinch of salt and some fresh chopped mint.

1. Slice the onion into thin rings.
2. Heat 1 tablespoon of the oil in a sauté pan over medium-high heat. Add the onions and reduce the heat to medium-low. Cook for about 15 minutes, until golden brown. Transfer to a bowl and set aside.
3. Add the remaining 2 tablespoons oil to the pan. Add the cumin, coriander, red pepper flakes, paprika, and allspice. Toast for about a minute, stirring constantly.
4. Add the tomatoes and 2 cups (480 ml) hot water, stirring well. Stir in the macaroni, rice, and lentils.
5. Slice the jalapeño into thin rings and add to the pan.
6. Reduce the heat to low, cover the pan, and simmer for 10 minutes, until the liquid has reduced by half.
7. Add the vinegar and season to taste with salt and pepper. Simmer for another 5 minutes uncovered, stirring occasionally.
8. Serve hot, topped with the browned onions.

BROCCOLI! BROCCOLI! BROCCOLI! BROCCOLI!

THAI BROCCOLI SALAD

WITH TOASTED SESAME

PREPARATION TIME 20 minutes • SERVES 4

Broccoli is a total superfood!
Plus, it tastes great—especially in this salad.

Salt
1 head broccoli (about 9 ounces/250 g)
2 tablespoons sesame seeds
1 red bell pepper, stemmed and seeded
2 scallions
2 garlic cloves
1 thumb-sized piece ginger
1 teaspoon dark (toasted) sesame oil
3 tablespoons peanut oil
3 tablespoons white wine vinegar
1 tablespoon soy sauce
1 tablespoon sriracha
1 teaspoon agave syrup

1. Bring a pot of salted water to a boil. Fill a large bowl with cold water and ice to make an ice bath.
2. Cut the broccoli into small florets. Peel and thinly slice the stems.
3. Blanch the broccoli for about 4 minutes, until bright green, then plunge in an ice bath to stop it from cooking. When the broccoli is cool, drain.
4. Toast the sesame seeds in a dry pan over medium-high heat for about 4 minutes, stirring constantly, until golden brown. Set aside.
5. Cut the bell pepper and scallions into thin strips. Mince the garlic. Grate the ginger.
6. Whisk together the sesame and peanut oils, the vinegar, soy sauce, sriracha, agave syrup, ½ teaspoon salt, the garlic, and ginger in a large bowl. Add the broccoli, bell pepper, and scallions and toss with the dressing.
7. Top with the toasted sesame seeds and serve.

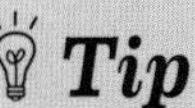

We love bringing this salad to barbecues, picnics, or the beach. If you like your food a little spicier, add a thinly sliced red chile.

BUTTERNUT SQUASH SALAD
WITH DUKKAH

PREPARATION 30 minutes • BAKING TIME 45 minutes • SERVES 4

We love the nutty flavor of butternut squash, especially when seasoned with dukkah, a North African mix of nuts and spices.

- 1 small butternut squash (about 1 pound/450 g)
- ¼ cup (60 ml) olive oil
- 3 garlic cloves
- 1 red jalapeño or other fresh chile
- ½ bunch fresh parsley
- 1¼ cups (250 g) instant couscous
- 1¾ cups (420 ml) boiling water
- 1 cup (160 g) drained cooked chickpeas
- Juice of 1 small lemon
- 3 tablespoons Dukkah (page 195)

1. Preheat the oven to 350°F (180°C). Line a baking sheet with parchment paper.
2. Peel the squash, then halve it lengthwise and remove the seeds. Brush the cut sides with 1 tablespoon of the oil and place it cut side down on the baking sheet. Roast for 45 minutes, or until fork-tender.
3. While the squash is roasting, mince the garlic and jalapeño. Coarsely chop the parsley.
4. Combine the garlic and chile with the couscous in a large bowl. Cover with the boiling water and then cover with a plate or dish towel for 10 minutes.
5. Remove the squash from the oven. When it's cool enough to handle, scoop the flesh from the skin with a large spoon. Cut into bite-sized pieces.
6. Fluff the couscous with a fork. Mix in the squash and chickpeas.
7. Whisk together the remaining 3 tablespoons olive oil, the lemon juice, parsley, and dukkah. Toss with the couscous mixture. Serve.

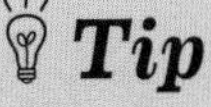

In this recipe we don't use the skin of the squash, but in other dishes, like a stir-fry, you can leave the skin on.

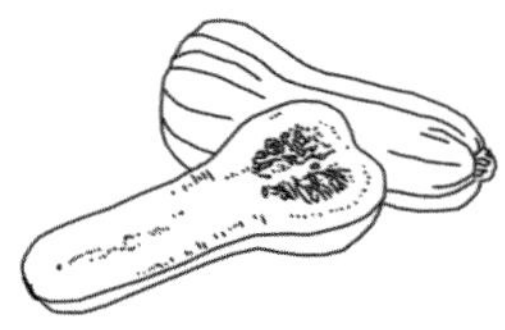

WINTER MINESTRONE

A WARMING TAKE ON THE CLASSIC

PREPARATION TIME 15 minutes • COOKING TIME 30 minutes • SERVES 4

Minestrone is a hearty soup, perfect for long winter evenings. Our version is also a great way to use up the ends of vegetables in your fridge.

- ½ bunch Swiss chard (5 ounces/150 g)
- 5 ounces (150 g) cabbage
- 1 onion
- 2 carrots, peeled
- ¼ cup (60 ml) olive oil
- 1 teaspoon dried thyme
- 1 teaspoon dried oregano
- ½ teaspoon ground cinnamon
- ¼ teaspoon ground cloves
- 1 quart (1 liter) vegetable broth
- One 14.5-ounce (411 g) can diced tomatoes
- 1½ cups (150 g) ditalini or other small macaroni
- ½ cup (100 g) drained canned cranberry or cannellini beans
- Salt and freshly ground black pepper

1. Cut the chard (including the stems) and cabbage into thin strips. Dice the onion. Slice the carrot into thin coins.
2. Heat the oil in a large pot over medium-high heat. Add the onion and cook until translucent, about 4 minutes.
3. Add the thyme, oregano, cinnamon, and cloves and stir well. Add the carrots, chard, and cabbage and cook for 5 minutes, stirring frequently.
4. Add the broth, tomatoes, and ditalini. Bring to a boil, then reduce the heat to low and cover the pot. Simmer for 20 minutes, or until the ditalini is al dente and the greens are tender.
5. Add the beans. Cook for 3 minutes more, until the beans are heated through. Season to taste with salt and pepper and serve.

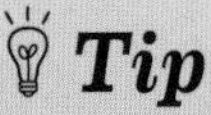

Tip

To make this minestrone even more Italian, serve with freshly made Focaccia (page 177). But any good bread will do.

This recipe is also great with Vegan Parmesan (page 69).

HOT 'N' SOUR SOUP

HOT, SWEET, SOUR, SPICY!

PREPARATION TIME 10 minutes • COOKING TIME 25 minutes • SERVES 8

We don't go out for Chinese food much anymore, but when we did, we would always order hot and sour soup. We never found a vegan version, so we developed our own recipe, which is super easy and tastes just as good.

- 4 dried wood ear or shiitake mushrooms
- 1 red jalapeño or other fresh red chile
- 2 quarts (2 L) vegetable broth
- ¼ cup plus 3 tablespoons (105 ml) soy sauce
- ⅓ cup (75 ml) rice vinegar
- 2 tablespoons tomato paste
- 1 tablespoon agave syrup
- ⅓ cup (40 g) tapioca starch
- 1 red bell pepper, stemmed and seeded
- 1 large carrot, peeled
- ½ cup (75 g) drained canned bamboo shoots
- ⅔ cup (50 g) fresh oyster mushrooms
- 2½ ounces (75 g) firm tofu
- ¾ cup (75 g) fresh bean sprouts
- 1 small bundle (2 ounces/50 g) glass noodles
- Salt and freshly ground black pepper

GLUTEN FREE

1. Place the dried mushrooms in a small heatproof bowl. Cover with boiling water and set aside for 10 minutes to rehydrate.
2. Finely mince the jalapeño.
3. Bring the broth, soy sauce, vinegar, tomato paste, agave syrup, and jalapeño to a boil in a large pot over high heat.
4. Whisk together the tapioca starch and ½ cup (120 ml) cold water in a small bowl. Whisk the starch slurry into the broth, stirring constantly.
5. Drain the mushrooms and discard the soaking water. Cut the bell pepper, carrot, bamboo shoots, and rehydrated mushrooms into thin strips. Tear the oyster mushrooms into bite-sized pieces. Crumble the tofu.
6. Add the vegetables, tofu, and noodles to the soup. Reduce the heat to medium and cook for 25 minutes. Season to taste with salt and pepper and serve hot.

SUSHI BOWL

VEGAN SUSHI FOR LAZYBONES

PREPARATION TIME 25 minutes • SERVES 4

Vegan sushi is one of our absolute favorite meals! But it definitely takes some effort to make. This is a simple and fast recipe for a quick meal.

FOR THE SUSHI

2 cups (400 g) sushi rice

2 carrots, peeled

1 green bell pepper, stemmed and seeded

1 avocado

½ medium cucumber

2 tablespoons sesame seeds

1 sheet nori

Parsley, to serve

FOR THE DRESSING

1 thumb-sized piece ginger

⅓ cup (75 ml) rice vinegar

2 tablespoons dark (toasted) sesame oil

2 tablespoons soy sauce

2 pinches of wasabi powder

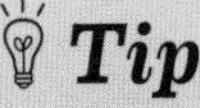

Tip

If you can't find sushi rice, any short-grain rice will do. If you choose short-grain brown rice, make sure you account for a longer cooking time. Different types of rice will give your sushi bowl slightly different flavors.

1. To make the sushi, combine the rice and 2 cups (480 ml) water in a medium saucepan and bring to a boil. Reduce the heat to low, cover, and cook for 15 minutes. Remove from the heat and let stand, covered, for 10 minutes.
2. Cut the carrots and bell pepper into thin strips. Cut the avocado into ½-inch (13 mm) slices. Cut the cucumber into 3-inch (7.5 cm) strips.
3. To make the dressing, grate the ginger into a small bowl, add the vinegar, sesame oil, soy sauce, and wasabi powder, and whisk together. Set aside.
4. Toast the sesame seeds in a dry pan over medium-high heat for about 4 minutes, until golden brown, stirring constantly.
5. Divide the rice among four bowls. Distribute the carrots, bell peppers, avocado, and cucumber over the rice. Drizzle with the dressing.
6. Using kitchen shears, cut the nori into thin strips. Top the bowls with the nori and the toasted sesame seeds. Garnish with parsley and serve immediately.

JAMBALAYA
WITH TEMPEH & SMOKED PAPRIKA

PREPARATION TIME 15 minutes • MARINATING TIME 4 hours
COOKING TIME 40 minutes • SERVES 4

We love the hearty flavors of Creole cuisine from Louisiana, especially jambalaya. Easily adaptable, smoky, spicy, and just plain tasty, this dish is a great way to use up vegetables hanging out in the fridge.

- 8 ounces (227 g) tempeh
- 1 garlic clove
- 1 tablespoon liquid smoke
- 1 teaspoon maple syrup
- ½ teaspoon salt
- 2 onions
- 4 stalks celery
- 3 red bell peppers, stemmed and seeded
- 1 red jalapeño or other fresh red chile
- ¼ cup (60 ml) olive oil
- ¼ cup (40 g) Creole Seasoning (see Tip)
- 1 tablespoon smoked paprika
- 1⅔ cups (300 g) brown rice
- One 14.5-ounce (411 g) can diced tomatoes
- 2 cups (480 ml) vegetable broth
- 1 tablespoon agave syrup
- Salt and freshly ground black pepper
- Parsley, to serve

1. Cut the tempeh into 1½-inch (4 cm) cubes. Mince the garlic. Put the garlic in a medium bowl with the liquid smoke, maple syrup, and salt. Mix well. Add the tempeh, stir to coat, cover the bowl, and marinate for 4 hours in the refrigerator, stirring after 2 hours.
2. Cut the onion, celery, and bell peppers into ¾-inch (20 mm) pieces. Finely chop the jalapeño.
3. Heat the oil in a saucepan over medium-high heat. Drain the tempeh and add to the oil with the Creole seasoning. Sauté for 5 minutes, or until golden brown.
4. Add the onion and jalapeño and cook for another 3 minutes, until softened.
5. Add the bell peppers, celery, paprika, rice, tomatoes, broth, and agave syrup. Stir and bring to a boil. Reduce the heat to medium-low and cook for 30 minutes, or until the rice is tender and the liquid has reduced. Season to taste with salt and pepper, garnish with parsley, and serve hot.

Tip

For homemade Creole Seasoning, combine 1 tablespoon onion powder, 1 tablespoon garlic powder, 1 tablespoon salt, 2 teaspoons freshly ground black pepper, 2 teaspoons ground white pepper, 2 teaspoons ground cayenne, 2 teaspoons dried thyme, and 2 teaspoons dried oregano.

ROASTED SQUASH SOUP

BOLLYWOOD STYLE

PREPARATION TIME 20 minutes • ROASTING TIME 20 minutes • SERVES 4

This Indian-inspired squash soup with roasted garlic is just the thing for a rainy fall day. The warming spices and creamy coconut milk give it an amazing flavor.

- 1½ pounds (750 g) red kuri or kabocha squash
- 2 medium russet potatoes
- 1 onion
- 1 carrot, peeled
- 3 tablespoons canola oil
- 1 teaspoon ground fennel seeds
- 1 teaspoon ground cumin
- 1 teaspoon red pepper flakes
- ½ teaspoon ground cinnamon
- Salt and freshly ground black pepper
- 4 garlic cloves, skin on
- 1 quart (1 L) vegetable broth
- ¾ cup (180 ml) full-fat coconut milk
- Parsley, to serve

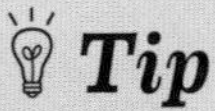

Tip

Serve our wonderful Dinner Rolls (page 173) or moist Garlic Naan (page 167) with this soup for a filling meal.

1. Preheat the oven to 400°F (200°C). Line a baking sheet with parchment paper.
2. Cut the squash in half and remove the seeds. Cut the squash and potatoes into large chunks. Coarsely chop the onion and carrot.
3. Mix together the oil, fennel, cumin, red pepper flakes, cinnamon, and ½ teaspoon salt in a large bowl. Add the squash, potatoes, onion, carrot, and garlic cloves and stir to coat.
4. Spread on the prepared baking sheet in an even layer. Roast for 20 minutes, stirring once after 10 minutes, until tender. Remove from the oven.
5. Pour the vegetable broth into a large pot over medium-high heat. Squeeze the soft roasted garlic out of the skins into the broth, then add the other roasted vegetables. Bring to a boil.
6. Add the coconut milk and simmer for 5 minutes. Using an immersion blender, purée the soup in the pot until smooth. Season to taste with salt and pepper. Garnish with parsley and serve immediately.

COOKING FOR FRIENDS & FAMILY

MEXICAN PAELLA

RICE WITH A TWIST

PREPARATION TIME 40 minutes • SERVES 4

What happens when you combine paella, the Spanish classic, with typically Mexican flavors? You end up with a rustic, savory rice dish that no one can resist.

- 1 red bell pepper, stemmed and seeded
- 1 yellow bell pepper, stemmed and seeded
- 1 medium tomato
- 5 ounces (150 g) baby bella (cremini) mushrooms
- 1 jalapeño
- 3 garlic cloves
- 2 tablespoons olive oil
- 7 ounces (200 g) green beans
- 2 tablespoons dried oregano
- 1½ teaspoons coriander seeds
- 2 tablespoons tequila
- 1⅓ cups (250 g) short-grain brown rice
- Pinch of saffron threads
- ⅓ cup (75 ml) boiling water
- ¾ cup (120 g) drained canned artichoke hearts
- Salt and freshly ground black pepper
- ¼ bunch fresh cilantro, chopped
- 1 avocado, seeded, peeled, and cubed
- 2 limes, quartered

1. Cut the bell peppers and tomato into chunks. Slice the mushrooms and jalapeño. Mince the garlic.
2. Heat the oil in a large sauté pan over medium-high heat. Add the bell peppers, tomato, mushrooms, jalapeño, garlic, green beans, oregano, and coriander seeds and sauté for 5 minutes, until softened.
3. Stir in the tequila. Add the rice and 2 cups (480 ml) water.
4. Place the saffron in a small bowl and add the boiling water. Let sit for a minute, then add to the pan. Reduce the heat to low, cover, and simmer for 25 minutes, until fragrant.
5. Quarter the artichokes. Stir into the paella. Simmer for 3 minutes to warm through.
6. Season to taste with salt and pepper. Serve hot, topped with the cilantro and avocado, with lime wedges on the side.

THAI BURGERS

SESAME-TOFU PATTIES WITH PEANUT SAUCE

PREPARATION TIME 25 minutes • COOKING TIME 10 minutes • SERVES 4

When your everyday life gets to be too much, escape to Thailand with these burgers!

FOR THE BURGERS

14 ounces (400 g) firm tofu, pressed (see Tip)

1 garlic clove

1 thumb-sized piece ginger, coarsely chopped

1 fresh red chile, stemmed and chopped

2 makrut lime leaves, torn

3 tablespoons soy sauce

2 tablespoons tomato paste

¼ bunch fresh cilantro, chopped

1 cup (100 g) bread crumbs

3 tablespoons cornstarch

2 tablespoons sesame seeds

¼ cup (60 ml) canola oil

FOR THE PEANUT SAUCE

⅓ cup (80 g) natural peanut butter

¼ cup plus 3 tablespoons (105 ml) full-fat coconut milk

½ teaspoon ground cayenne

1 teaspoon salt

FOR SERVING

1 medium tomato

4 burger buns

4 romaine lettuce leaves

3½ ounces (100 g) red cabbage, thinly sliced (about 1 cup)

1. To make the burgers, purée half of the tofu, the garlic, ginger, chile, lime leaves, soy sauce, tomato paste, and cilantro in a food processor.
2. Crumble the remaining tofu and mix into the purée. Add the bread crumbs and cornstarch and mix well.
3. Shape the mixture into 4 burgers. Roll in the sesame seeds, coating both sides.
4. Place a sauté pan over medium heat and add the oil. Cook the burgers until golden brown on both sides, about 5 minutes on each side.
5. While the burgers are cooking, make the sauce. Place the peanut butter, coconut milk, cayenne, and salt in a small saucepan over medium heat and whisk until smooth. When warmed through, remove from the heat.
6. Slice the tomato. Toast the buns.
7. Top a bun bottom with a lettuce leaf, some cabbage, a burger, peanut sauce, and a slice of tomato. Cover with the bun top and serve.

Tip

Be sure to remove excess liquid from the tofu so the burgers won't fall apart. Wrap the block of tofu in a few layers of paper towels or a clean dish towel. Place a flat, heavy object on top and press for at least 20 minutes before using.

savoy cabbage
+ noodles
+ French
sage sauce

SAVOY NOODLES

A SHEET-PAN DINNER WITH SAGE SAUCE

PREPARATION TIME 20 minutes • BAKING TIME 20 minutes • SERVES 4

Savoy cabbage is beloved for its delicate flavor. When combined with chewy noodles and a silky sage sauce, it's a little bit of Alsace on your plate.

- Salt and freshly ground black pepper
- 1 pound (450 g) fusilli or penne
- 14 ounces (400 g) savoy cabbage
- 1 tablespoon olive oil
- 1 onion
- 2 garlic cloves
- Handful of sage leaves
- 2 tablespoons vegan butter
- 1 tablespoon all-purpose flour
- 1 cup (240 ml) oat milk or oat cream
- 1¼ cups (300 ml) vegetable broth
- 3 tablespoons white wine
- 1 teaspoon mustard

1. Preheat the oven to 300°F (140°C). Line a baking sheet with parchment paper.
2. Bring a large pot of salted water to a boil. Add the pasta and cook until not quite al dente, about 8 minutes.
3. While the pasta is cooking, slice the cabbage into thin strips. Just before the noodles are finished cooking, throw the cabbage into the cooking water to blanch.
4. As soon as the pasta is al dente, drain it and the cabbage in a colander. Drizzle with the oil and toss to coat. Spread in an even layer on the prepared baking sheet. Bake for 20 minutes, stirring once after 10 minutes, until browned and tender.
5. While the pasta is baking, finely dice the onion. Mince the garlic and sage.
6. Melt the vegan butter in a small saucepan over medium heat. Add the onion and cook until translucent, about 3 minutes. Add the sage, garlic, and flour. Cook for another minute, stirring constantly.
7. Whisk in the milk, broth, and wine. Bring to a boil briefly, then reduce the heat to low. Whisk in the mustard and add salt and pepper to taste. Let simmer for another 10 minutes.
8. Remove the pasta and cabbage from the oven and transfer to a bowl. Drizzle the sauce over the pasta and cabbage and serve.

Tip

You can make this filling winter dish even heartier by adding small cubes of smoked tofu to the sage sauce. You can also swap out the savoy cabbage for regular cabbage or curly kale.

Wild herbs:
nettles
bishop's weed (goutweed)
sorrel
dandelion
ramps

SPINACH STRUDEL

WITH WILD HERBS

PREPARATION TIME 20 minutes • BAKING TIME 20 minutes • SERVES 4

Like arugula before them, wild greens such as nettles, sorrel, and bishop's weed (goutweed) are often considered weeds and can be hard to find in supermarkets. But we hope they find their place in the sun soon! If you are unable to find or forage these greens, you can replace them with spinach or dandelion greens.

- 1 medium onion
- 1 carrot, peeled
- 1 russet potato, peeled
- 2 garlic cloves
- 5 ounces (150 g) firm tofu
- 2 tablespoons olive oil
- 3½ cups (150 g) mixed wild greens (such as nettles, sorrel, or bishop's weed), packed
- 12 ounces (350 g) fresh spinach
- 3 teaspoons herbes de Provence
- 2 teaspoons lemon juice
- 2 teaspoons mustard
- 3 tablespoons nutritional yeast
- Salt and freshly ground black pepper
- One 10 × 15-inch (25 × 40 cm) sheet puff pastry, thawed

1. Preheat the oven to 350°F (180°C). Line a baking sheet with parchment paper.
2. Finely dice the onion, carrot, and potato. Mince the garlic. Crumble the tofu.
3. Heat the oil in a sauté pan over high heat. Sauté the carrot, potato, and crumbled tofu for 5 minutes, stirring frequently.
4. Reduce to medium heat and add the onion, wild greens, spinach, garlic, herbes de Provence, lemon juice, mustard, and nutritional yeast. Cook for 5 minutes, stirring frequently, until the greens begin to wilt. Remove from the heat and season to taste with salt and pepper. Let cool briefly.
5. Roll out the puff pastry to about ⅛ inch (3 mm) thick on the prepared baking sheet.
6. Place the filling lengthwise down the middle of the pastry sheet, leaving a small border at the short ends. Fold the short ends over the filling. Fold one long side over the filling, then fold the other long side over that pastry. Press the seam gently to adhere. Flip the folded pastry over so that the seam is against the pan. Cut a few slits into the top of the pastry.
7. Bake for 20 minutes, or until golden brown. Serve warm.

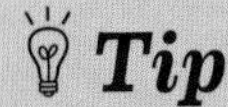

Tip

Get creative with your strudel fillings! Use your favorite vegetables to make the strudel your own.

SEITAN FAJITAS

VEGAN TEX-MEX

PREPARATION TIME 30 minutes • SERVES 4

It's hard for some to imagine Tex-Mex dishes like fajitas, burritos, and tacos without meat, but we love these seitan fajitas packed with tasty vegetables.

- 7 ounces (200g) seitan
- 1 red bell pepper, stemmed and seeded
- 1 yellow bell pepper, stemmed and seeded
- 1 onion
- 2 garlic cloves
- 4 tablespoons olive oil
- 1¼ cups (200 g) drained cooked kidney beans
- 1 teaspoon ground cumin
- ½ teaspoon dried oregano
- ¼ bunch fresh cilantro
- Salt and freshly ground black pepper
- 4 large flour tortillas
- 1 tablespoon drained sliced pickled jalapeño
- 1 lime, quartered

1. Slice the seitan, bell peppers, and onion into strips. Finely mince the garlic.
2. Heat 2 tablespoons of the oil in a sauté pan over medium-high heat. Add the seitan and sauté for about 8 minutes, stirring frequently, until golden brown. Transfer to a plate, cover to keep warm, and set aside.
3. Add the remaining 2 tablespoons oil to the pan and reduce the heat to medium. Sauté the bell peppers and onion for about 8 minutes, stirring occasionally, until softened.
4. Add the beans, cumin, and oregano. Reduce the heat to medium-low and simmer for about 5 minutes to heat through.
5. Coarsely chop the cilantro. Add the cilantro and garlic to the pan. Stir well and season to taste with salt and pepper.
6. Warm the tortillas in a dry pan over medium-high heat.
7. Spoon some of the vegetable mixture onto each tortilla. Top with the seitan and jalapeños. Serve with the lime wedges.

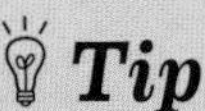

Tip

We love serving our Pico de Gallo (page 181) with these fajitas, along with guacamole and soy yogurt.

HASH BROWNS
WITH HERBED TZATZIKI

PREPARATION TIME 15 minutes • FRYING TIME 15 minutes • MAKES 8 patties

Traditional hash browns are pretty high in calories. We developed this lighter version made with parsnips and onions and served with a fresh herbed tzatziki.

FOR THE TZATZIKI

¼ medium cucumber
1 garlic clove
2 tablespoons fresh parsley leaves, plus more to serve
1 cup (250 g) plain soy yogurt
1 tablespoon olive oil
Salt and freshly ground black pepper

FOR THE HASH BROWNS

12 ounces (400 g) russet potatoes
9 ounces (250 g) parsnips
1 medium onion
3 tablespoons cornstarch
2 tablespoons olive oil

1. To make the tzatziki, grate the cucumber and squeeze out some of the excess water. Crush and chop the garlic. Finely chop the parsley.
2. Combine the cucumber, garlic, and parsley with the yogurt and oil in a bowl. Season to taste with salt and pepper. Set aside.
3. To make the hash browns, finely grate the potatoes, parsnips, and onion into a large bowl. Season with salt and let sit for 5 minutes.
4. Drain the potato mixture and squeeze out any excess liquid by hand. Return to the bowl.
5. Add the cornstarch and mix well with two forks. Shape into 8 patties.
6. Heat the oil in a large sauté pan over medium-high heat. Fry the hash browns for about 4 minutes on each side, until golden.
7. Serve the piping-hot hash browns with the tzatziki and extra parsley on top.

Tip

Try making the hash browns with other vegetables, such as zucchini, carrots, pumpkin, or even beets. Breakfast will never be boring again!

Yum!

ETHIOPIAN CHARD & KALE WOT

WITH INJERA BREAD

PREPARATION TIME 15 minutes • FERMENTING TIME 24 hours
COOKING TIME 25 minutes • SERVES 4

Our take on the Ethiopian classic stew is made with Swiss chard and curly kale, and served with homemade injera flatbreads. Double the recipe to share with a group of friends and family.

FOR THE INJERA

- 2⅔ cups (300 g) teff flour
- 2¼ teaspoons (1 packet) instant yeast

FOR THE WOT

- 1 large onion
- 1 thumb-sized piece ginger
- 1 green jalapeño
- 1 serrano chile
- 3 garlic cloves
- 14 ounces (400 g) Swiss chard
- 14 ounces (400 g) curly kale
- 2 tablespoons peanut oil
- Salt and freshly ground black pepper

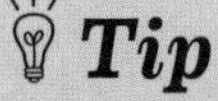

Tip

Minted Soy Yogurt (page 65) is a tasty accompaniment to the wot. To make a small amount, mix plain soy yogurt with fresh mint, salt, and pepper, or try one of your favorite seasonings.

1. To start the injera, whisk the teff flour, yeast, and 3¼ cups (780 ml) water in a large bowl. Cover with a dish towel. Let the batter sit at least 24 hours at room temperature to ferment.
2. To prepare the wot, finely mince the onion, ginger, jalapeño, serrano chile, and garlic. Chop the chard and kale into bite-sized pieces.
3. Heat the oil in a sauté pan over high heat. Add the onion, ginger, chile, and garlic. Sauté for a few minutes, stirring frequently, until softened.
4. Add the chopped greens, season to taste, and sauté for another 3 minutes. Pour in 3½ tablespoons water and reduce the heat to medium. Cover and simmer for about 15 minutes, stirring occasionally, until softened.
5. Meanwhile, carefully pour off any water on the surface of the injera batter. Mix well.
6. Heat a dry nonstick sauté pan over medium-high heat. Pour in a ladle of injera batter, allowing it to spread thin. Cook for 1 minute, then cover with a lid and cook for another 2 minutes, until holes appear on the surface. Transfer to a plate. Repeat until the batter is gone.
7. Serve the wot on the injera.

MOROCCAN STEW

WITH BLACK-EYED PEAS & FRESH HERBS

PREPARATION TIME 10 minutes • SOAKING TIME 12 hours or overnight
COOKING TIME About 1 hour • SERVES 4

This hearty stew can be eaten at any time of year. It's light yet filling and has a wonderfully savory aroma.

1¼ cups (250 g) dried black-eyed peas
1 pound (500 g) tomatoes
1 large onion
3 garlic cloves
1 thumb-sized piece ginger
2 tablespoons fresh parsley leaves
2 tablespoons fresh cilantro leaves
2 tablespoons tomato paste
2 tablespoons olive oil
2 teaspoons ground cumin
2 teaspoons ground paprika
1½ teaspoons ground cayenne
2 bay leaves
Salt
Parsley, to serve

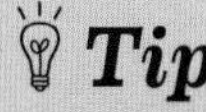

1. Place the black-eyed peas in a medium bowl and cover with water. Soak at least 12 hours or overnight.
2. Cut the tomatoes into a large dice. Finely chop the onion, garlic, ginger, parsley, and cilantro.
3. Drain the black-eyed peas. Put them in a large pot and add the tomatoes, onion, garlic, ginger, parsley, cilantro, tomato paste, oil, cumin, paprika, cayenne, bay leaves, and 3½ cups (840 ml) water. Bring to a boil, cover, then reduce to a simmer for 1 hour, or until the black-eyed peas are tender.
4. Remove the bay leaves, season to taste with salt, top with parsley, and serve hot.

Tip

Serve our Moroccan Stew with homemade Harissa (page 195) and freshly made Flatbread (page 169).

Delicious & beautiful!

SUPER BEAN BURGERS

WHO'S YOUR PATTY?

PREPARATION TIME 40 minutes • RESTING TIME 2 hours • SERVES 4

"I'm lovin' it;" "Think outside the bun;" "Finger-lickin' good"— all of these fast-food slogans apply to our super smoky bean burger. One of our absolute favorites!

FOR THE PATTIES

1 tablespoon ground flaxseed

1 medium onion

2 garlic cloves

¼ cup (60 ml) olive oil

Salt and freshly ground black pepper

One 15-ounce (425 g) can black beans, drained

1 medium beet, boiled until soft, peeled, and cut into large chunks

¼ cup (50 g) cooked brown rice

3 tablespoons oat flour

1 teaspoon mustard

1½ teaspoons smoked paprika

½ teaspoon ground cumin

½ teaspoon dried thyme

FOR SERVING

4 burger buns

4 tablespoons ketchup

4 lettuce leaves

4 slices vegan cheese

1. To make the patties, whisk the flaxseed with 3 tablespoons water in a small bowl. Set aside.
2. Finely dice the onion. Mince the garlic.
3. Heat 1 tablespoon of the oil in a small pan over high heat. Reduce the heat to low and add the onion with ¼ teaspoon salt. Cook for about 10 minutes, until softened.
4. Add the garlic. Cook for another 2 minutes, until fragrant. Remove from the heat.
5. Put half of the beans and the beet in a food processor and coarsely chop. Transfer to a bowl and stir in the remaining beans, the onion and garlic, rice, oat flour, mustard, paprika, cumin, and thyme. Season to taste with salt and pepper. Cover and refrigerate for 2 hours.
6. Shape into 4 patties. Heat the remaining 3 tablespoons olive oil in a large sauté pan over medium-high heat. Cook the burgers until crisp, for about 5 minutes on each side.
7. To serve, spread the buns with ketchup. Layer each bun with a lettuce leaf, patty, and a slice of cheese.

CAULIFLOWER STEAKS
WITH TOMATO-MINT RICE

PREPARATION TIME 15 minutes • COOKING TIME 25 minutes • SERVES 4

Cauliflower can get a bad rap as a boring vegetable. But we think it tastes amazing raw, grated into a salad, or fried with various seasonings. It's especially delicious in this wonderfully moist tomato-mint rice dish.

FOR THE CAULIFLOWER STEAKS

1 large head cauliflower (2 pounds/450 g)

¼ cup (60 ml) olive oil

2 teaspoons ground cumin

1 teaspoon ground coriander

1 teaspoon ground cayenne

½ teaspoon salt

1 teaspoon agave syrup

1 lemon, quartered

FOR THE TOMATO-MINT RICE

1⅓ cups (250 g) long-grain white rice

Half of a 14.5-ounce (411 g) can diced tomatoes

1 teaspoon tomato paste

1 garlic clove

½ teaspoon salt

1 tablespoon agave syrup

1 tablespoon fresh mint leaves

1 lemon, quartered

1. Preheat the oven to 350°F (180°C). Line a baking sheet with parchment paper.
2. Cut the cauliflower vertically into steaks ½ inch (13 mm) thick.
3. Heat 2 tablespoons of the oil in a sauté pan over high heat. Sear the cauliflower steaks for 4 minutes on each side. As they are done, transfer them to the baking sheet.
4. In a small bowl, whisk together the remaining 2 tablespoons oil, the cumin, coriander, cayenne, salt, and agave syrup. Brush the cauliflower liberally on both sides with the glaze.
5. Bake for 15 minutes, flipping halfway through.
6. While the cauliflower steaks are baking, combine the rice, 1 cup (240 ml) water, tomatoes, tomato paste, garlic, salt, and agave syrup to a small saucepan over high heat and bring to a boil. Reduce the heat to low, cover, and simmer for 15 minutes.
7. Finely mince the mint and fold into the cooked rice. Serve the cauliflower steaks with the rice and lemon wedges.

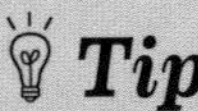

These steaks are even better topped with soy yogurt mixed with chopped fresh herbs like parsley or more mint (see Minted Soy Yogurt, page 65).

PIZZA MARRAKESH

A WHOLE NEW WORLD OF PIZZA

PREPARATION TIME 25 minutes • MAKES 4 pizzas

Instead of sauce and cheese, this pizza is topped with a creamy North African–inspired sauce made with white beans and fresh parsley.

One 15-ounce (425 g) can white beans, drained
2 garlic cloves
1 small bunch fresh parsley
¾ teaspoon ground paprika
1½ teaspoon ground cumin
Juice of 1 lemon
Salt
2 red onions
4 green bell peppers, stemmed and seeded
Flour, for rolling
⅓ cup (75 g) cured black olives, pitted
Basic Pizza Dough (page 165)

1. Preheat the oven to 450°F (230°C). Line two baking sheets with parchment paper.
2. Combine the beans, garlic, parsley, spices, and lemon juice in a food processor and pulse until smooth. Season to taste with salt.
3. Slice the red onions into thin rings. Slice the bell peppers.
4. Divide the dough into four pieces. Roll out each on a well-floured surface until it is a round about ½ inch (13 mm) thick. Transfer to the baking sheets.
5. Spread the bean sauce in an even layer on the pizzas. Top with the onion, bell peppers, and olives.
6. Bake for 10 to 12 minutes, until the crust is lightly brown. Serve hot.

GOAN WRAPS

WITH YELLOW LENTIL HUMMUS

PREPARATION TIME 15 minutes • COOKING TIME 45 minutes • SERVES 4

Want a little Indian vibe in your kitchen? Our filling wraps are great energy boosters with rich Indian flavors. These are a great meal for when you're on the go, traveling to work or to school.

FOR THE YELLOW LENTIL HUMMUS

½ cup (100 g) yellow lentils (*mung dal*) or yellow split peas

½ teaspoon ground cumin

1 teaspoon lemon juice

Salt and freshly ground black pepper

FOR THE FILLING

1 medium onion

2 medium russet potatoes

2 garlic cloves

2 tablespoons peanut oil

2 teaspoons curry power

1 teaspoon mustard seeds

1 teaspoon ground ginger

1 teaspoon ground coriander

1 cup (125 g) small cauliflower florets

2 medium tomatoes

2 teaspoons agave syrup

Salt and freshly ground black pepper

FOR THE WRAPS

4 large flour tortillas

¼ bunch fresh cilantro, chopped

SOY FREE

1. To make the hummus, combine the lentils with 1½ cups (360 ml) water in a small saucepan. Bring to a boil over medium-high heat, then reduce the heat to low and simmer until soft, about 30 minutes. Remove from the heat and let cool a bit.

2. Purée the lentils in a food processor with the cumin and lemon juice. Season to taste with salt and pepper and set aside.

3. To make the filling, finely dice the onion and potatoes. Thinly slice the garlic.

4. Pour the oil into a saucepan over medium-high heat. Add the curry powder, mustard seeds, ginger, and coriander and cook, stirring constantly, for a minute or two, until fragrant.

5. Add the cauliflower, potatoes, onions, and garlic. Sauté for 4 minutes, until softened.

6. Dice the tomatoes and add to the vegetables along with the agave syrup. Reduce the heat to low and let simmer for 10 minutes, until the tomatoes break down. Season to taste with salt and pepper.

7. While the filling is simmering, warm the tortillas in a dry pan over medium-high heat.

8. Spread the hummus on the warm tortillas, top with the filling, and sprinkle with the cilantro. Roll up and eat!

DATE-NIGHT DINNERS

BON APPÉTIT!

POTATO GALETTE
WITH LEEKS

PREPARATION TIME 20 minutes • BAKING TIME 50 minutes • MAKES one 11-inch (28 cm) galette

We love this healthy twist on a classic pommes Anna, *with crisp, thin slices of potato combined with juicy leeks and Provençal herbs. Try it and see!*

- 4 tablespoons olive oil
- 1 medium leek, trimmed and rinsed
- 3 garlic cloves
- Pinch of grated nutmeg
- 1 tablespoon herbes de Provence
- Salt and freshly ground black pepper
- 1¾ pounds (850 g) russet potatoes, peeled
- Chopped parsley, to serve

1. Preheat the oven to 400°F (200°C). Grease an 11-inch (28 cm) tart or springform pan with 1 tablespoon of the oil.
2. Thinly slice the white and light green parts of the leek. Thinly slice the garlic.
3. Pour 1 tablespoon of the oil into a sauté pan set over medium-high heat. Add the leeks and cook for about 3 minutes, stirring frequently, until softened. Add the garlic, nutmeg, and herbes de Provence. Season to taste with salt and pepper and cook for an additional 4 minutes, until fragrant. Remove from the heat.
4. Thinly slice the potatoes.
5. Place an even layer of one-third of the potatoes in the pan in slightly overlapping concentric circles. Drizzle with a little of the remaining oil. Spread half of the leeks over the potatoes. Season with salt and pepper.
6. Repeat Step 5. Finish with a top layer of potatoes and drizzle with any remaining oil. Cover the pan with aluminum foil and bake for 20 minutes.
7. Remove the foil and bake for another 30 minutes, until golden brown. Top with parsley and serve hot or at room temperature.

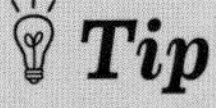

Tip

Alongside this elegant tart, we recommend serving some herbed soy yogurt (see Minted Soy Yogurt, page 65) or a fresh and crunchy side salad with radishes.

POTSTICKERS

ASIAN STREET FOOD AT HOME

PREPARATION TIME 1 hour • COOKING TIME 35 minutes • MAKES 32 potstickers

We enjoy all dim sum. But dumplings, especially potstickers, are our favorites. These deliciously filled dumplings, also known as gyoza *in Japan, are crisp on the outside and moist and chewy on the inside.*

FOR THE FILLING

3 dried shiitake mushrooms
7 ounces (200 g) firm tofu
1 carrot, peeled
1 scallion
1 thumb-sized piece ginger
1 garlic clove
1 tablespoon dark (toasted) sesame oil
1 tablespoon mirin
1 tablespoon soy sauce
1 teaspoon cornstarch
1 teaspoon agave syrup
2 tablespoons peanut oil
Yum Yum Sauce (page 195) or more soy sauce, for serving

FOR THE DOUGH

2⅓ cups plus 1 tablespoon (300 g) all-purpose flour
½ teaspoon salt

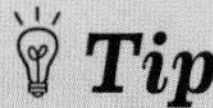

Tip

If you want to experiment, YouTube has a number of videos where you can learn different dumpling folding techniques.

1. To start the filling, place the shiitakes in a small bowl and cover with boiling water. Let sit for 30 minutes.
2. While the shiitakes are soaking, make the wrapper dough. Combine the flour, salt, and 1 cup (240 ml) hot water in a bowl. Knead until smooth. Let sit, covered, for 20 minutes.
3. Drain the shiitakes. Crumble the tofu. Finely grate the carrot. Thinly slice the scallions. Finely mince the ginger, garlic, and shiitakes.
4. Mix the shiitakes, tofu, carrot, scallions, ginger, garlic, sesame oil, mirin, soy sauce, cornstarch, and agave syrup in a bowl.
5. Divide the dough into 32 equal pieces. Roll out to rounds 1⁄16 inch (1.5 mm) thick. Place 1 heaping teaspoon filling in the middle of each wrapper. Working with one wrapper at a time, wet your fingers with warm water and dampen the dough around the filling. Fold the wrapper in half and crimp together the edges. Stand each potsticker on its fold.
6. Pour the peanut oil into a large sauté pan set over high heat. Place the potstickers on their folds, with the crimped edge up, in the pan. Reduce to medium-high and cook for about 6 minutes, until golden brown.
7. Add ½ cup (120 ml) hot water to the pan and cover. Let steam for 10 minutes.
8. Serve the potstickers with your choice of sauce.

BELUGA LENTIL CURRY

THAI STYLE

PREPARATION TIME 30 minutes • SERVES 4

Beluga lentils, like all other lentils, don't need to be soaked before cooking. They're wonderful in salads or as a versatile side dish. We think their nutty flavor is perfect in this Thai-inspired curry.

- 1 cup (200 g) beluga lentils
- 6 makrut lime leaves
- 1 carrot, peeled
- 1 green bell pepper, stemmed and seeded
- 2 scallions
- 4 cherry tomatoes
- 2 garlic cloves
- 1 thumb-sized piece ginger
- 1 serrano chile
- One 13.5-ounce (400 ml) can full-fat coconut milk
- ¼ cup (60 ml) soy sauce
- 3½ ounces (100 g) firm tofu
- 2 tablespoons peanut oil
- ½ cup (75 g) drained canned bamboo shoots
- ½ cup (50 g) fresh bean sprouts
- Steamed jasmine or basmati rice, for serving
- ¼ bunch fresh cilantro, chopped

Tip

Beluga lentils that have spent too much time on a supermarket shelf or in a pantry will take longer to cook. Test your lentils before draining them, and never mix older lentils with a new package.

1. Cook the lentils per the package instructions, adding 3 makrut lime leaves to the pot. Drain. Remove and discard the lime leaves.
2. Cut the carrot and bell pepper into thin strips. Thinly slice the scallion, keeping the green and white parts separate. Halve the tomatoes. Coarsely chop the garlic, ginger, and chile.
3. Finely purée the white part of the scallions, the garlic, ginger, chile, the remaining 3 lime leaves, the coconut milk, and soy sauce with an immersion blender or in a blender or food processor to make the sauce.
4. Cut the tofu into 1-inch (2.5 cm) cubes. Pour the oil into a large sauté pan over medium-high heat. Cook the tofu for 6 minutes, stirring occasionally, until golden brown.
5. Add the carrot, bell pepper, scallion greens, tomatoes, bamboo shoots, and bean sprouts, and stir-fry for another 5 minutes, until softened.
6. Add the coconut sauce, then stir in the lentils. Reduce the heat to low, cover, and let simmer for 10 minutes for everything to heat and the flavors to blend.
7. Serve over jasmine or basmati rice, topped with the chopped cilantro.

TAPENADE TARTLETS

WITH CHERRY TOMATOES

PREPARATION TIME 20 minutes • BAKING TIME 15 minutes • MAKES 6 tartlets

This dreamy French tapenade can be used in many ways—as a hearty spread, a dipping sauce for our Rosemary Crackers (page 47), or spread on top of crispy puff pastry tartlets.

- One 10 × 15-inch (25 × 40 cm) sheet puff pastry, thawed
- ⅓ cup (50 g) pitted Kalamata olives
- 1¾ ounces (50 g) smoked tofu
- 1 tablespoon olive oil
- ½ teaspoon dried thyme
- ¼ teaspoon dried oregano
- 1 teaspoon capers in brine, drained, plus 1 teaspoon of the brine
- Salt and freshly ground black pepper
- 1½ cups (200 g) cherry tomatoes
- 6 lettuce leaves

1. Preheat the oven to 350°F (180°C). Line a baking sheet with parchment paper.
2. Roll out the puff pastry on a lightly floured surface to ⅛ inch (3 mm) thick. Cut out six 4-inch (10 cm) rounds and fit each into a tartlet pan.
3. Purée the olives, smoked tofu, 2 teaspoons of the olive oil, the thyme, oregano, capers, and brine together in a blender or food processor until smooth. Season to taste with salt and pepper.
4. Divide the tapenade equally among the tartlet shells. Slice the cherry tomatoes and top the tartlets with the slices. Drizzle with the remaining 1 teaspoon olive oil.
5. Place the tartlet pans on the prepared baking sheet. Bake for 15 minutes, or until golden brown.
6. Remove from the oven and remove the tartlets from the pans. Arrange the lettuce on serving plates, place a tartlet on each, and serve immediately.

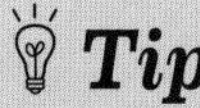

Tip

Any leftover puff pastry can be torn or cut into strips, seasoned, and twisted. Bake the strips with the tartlets and enjoy them as a no-waste bonus snack!

QUESADILLAS

VEGAN CHEESE FOR DAYS!

PREPARATION TIME 15 minutes • COOKING TIME 30 minutes • SERVES 4

You can enjoy this popular Mexican dish, made with our delicious vegan cheese sauce, at home whenever you like.

FOR THE CHEESE SAUCE

Salt

14 ounces (400 g) russet potatoes, peeled

1 large carrot, peeled

¼ cup plus 2 tablespoons (20 g) nutritional yeast

⅔ cup (100 g) raw cashews

1 garlic clove

1 red jalapeño or other fresh red chile, stemmed and seeded

Juice of ½ lemon

FOR THE QUESADILLAS

One 15-ounce (425 g) can pinto beans, drained

1 tablespoon dried oregano

Salt and freshly ground black pepper

8 large flour tortillas

FOR TOPPING

2 avocados

2 red jalapeños or other fresh red chiles

¼ bunch fresh cilantro

2 tablespoons sliced pickled jalapeños

1. To make the cheese sauce, bring a large pot of salted water to boil over high heat. Cut the potatoes and carrot into large chunks. Add to the boiling water and boil for about 15 minutes, until tender. Drain, then return to the pot.

2. Combine the potatoes, carrot, nutritional yeast, cashews, garlic, jalapeño, and lemon juice in a food processor. Purée until smooth. Return to the pot and bring to a boil over medium-high heat, then simmer for 2 minutes. Remove from the heat but keep warm.

3. To make the quesadillas, mash the beans with a fork and season with the oregano and salt and pepper to taste. Set aside.

4. Spread the cheese sauce on four of the tortillas, then layer with mashed beans. Top with the remaining tortillas.

5. Toast each quesadilla in a dry pan over medium-high heat for about 2 minutes per side.

6. While the quesadillas are toasting, prepare the toppings. Pit, peel, and cube the avocado. Thinly slice the jalapeños. Coarsely chop the cilantro.

7. Cut the quesadillas into wedges and top with the avocado, fresh and pickled jalapeños, and cilantro.

POLENTA LASAGNA

WITH LENTIL-LEEK RAGÙ

PREPARATION TIME 60 minutes • SERVES 4

This healthier version of lasagna replaces the pasta sheets with polenta and the meat ragù with nourishing lentils and leeks. If you like, you can top the lasagna with a few slices of vegan cheese.

FOR THE RAGÙ

- 1 leek, trimmed and rinsed
- 1 mild fresh chile
- 2 garlic cloves
- ½ red bell pepper, stemmed and seeded
- 2 tablespoons olive oil
- 1 teaspoon dried rosemary
- ¾ cup (150 g) green or brown lentils
- One 14.5-ounce (411 g) can diced tomatoes
- 2 bay leaves
- 1 tablespoon balsamic vinegar
- Salt and freshly ground black pepper

FOR THE POLENTA

- 1¼ cups (200 g) instant polenta
- 2 tablespoons chopped fresh parsley
- 3 tablespoons nutritional yeast
- 2 tablespoons olive oil
- 1 medium plum tomato

1. To make the ragù, slice the white and light green parts of the leek. Slice the chile. Finely chop the garlic. Dice the bell pepper.
2. Heat the oil in a large pot over medium heat. Add the leek, chile, garlic, bell pepper, and rosemary and sauté for 5 minutes, until softened.
3. Add the lentils, canned tomatoes, bay leaves, and 2 cups (480 ml) water. Bring to a boil. Reduce the heat to low, cover, and simmer for 20 minutes, until the lentils are soft.
4. Remove the ragù from the heat. Season with the vinegar and salt and pepper to taste.
5. Preheat the oven to 325°F (165°C).
6. To make the polenta, bring 2 cups (480 ml) water to a boil in a saucepan. Whisk in the polenta. Reduce the heat to medium-low and simmer, stirring frequently, for 15 minutes. Stir in the parsley and nutritional yeast, then season to taste.
7. Grease an 8-inch (20 cm) square baking pan with 1 tablespoon of the oil. Spread half the polenta in the pan. Distribute the ragù evenly over the polenta and layer the top with the remaining polenta.
8. Slice the plum tomato and scatter it over the polenta. Drizzle with the remaining tablespoon oil. Bake for 15 minutes, or until golden brown.

TAJ MAHAL SQUASH CURRY

WITH CHICKPEAS

PREPARATION TIME 10 minutes • COOKING TIME 30 minutes • SERVES 4

This curry is made entirely without ghee (Indian clarified butter) but is as good as anything you'll eat in an Indian restaurant.

- 1 pound (500 g) red kuri or kabocha squash
- 9 ounces (250 g) russet potatoes
- 2 onions
- 1 garlic clove
- 1 red jalapeño or other fresh red chile
- 3 tablespoons peanut oil
- One 13.5-ounce (400 ml) can full-fat coconut milk
- 3 tablespoons dried fenugreek leaves
- 1 tablespoon plus 1 teaspoon garam masala
- 1 teaspoon salt
- One 15-ounce (425 g) can chickpeas, drained
- 1 teaspoon grated lemon zest
- Juice of 1 lemon
- Steamed basmati rice or Garlic Naan (page 167), for serving

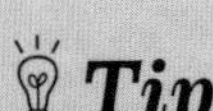

1. Cut the squash in half and remove the seeds. Cut the squash, potato, and onion into large chunks. Mince the garlic and jalapeño.
2. Heat the oil in a large pot over high heat. Sauté the squash, potatoes, and onions for about 4 minutes, stirring frequently, until slightly softened.
3. Add the garlic and jalapeño and sauté for a few minutes.
4. Add the coconut milk, fenugreek, garam masala, and salt. Bring to a boil, then reduce the heat to a simmer. Cook for 10 minutes, or until the vegetables are tender.
5. Add the chickpeas and simmer for another 10 minutes, until the liquid reduces slightly. Remove from the heat.
6. Stir in the lemon zest and juice.
7. Serve with the basmati rice or Garlic Naan.

Tip

Dried fenugreek can be found in Indian grocery stores or online. It lasts for a long time and is a very versatile ingredient used in many different curries.

FIVE-SPICE BAOZI

DELICIOUS STEAMED BUNS

PREPARATION TIME 25 minutes • PROOFING TIME 30 minutes
COOKING TIME 30 minutes • MAKES 16 dumplings

FOR THE DOUGH

About 1 teaspoon (½ packet) active dry yeast

2 cups (250 g) spelt flour, plus more for kneading

1 teaspoon salt

FOR THE FILLING

2 tablespoons dried wood ear or shiitake mushrooms

8 ounces (220 g) seitan

1 medium onion

1 garlic clove

2 tablespoons peanut oil

3 tablespoons five-spice powder

2 tablespoons soy sauce

1 teaspoon dark (toasted) sesame oil

1. To make the dough, whisk the yeast into 1/2 cup plus 2 tablespoons (150 ml) warm water. Let stand until the yeast has dissolved.
2. Mix together the flour and salt in a large bowl. Stir in the yeast until the flour is fully moistened.
3. Knead the dough on a floured work surface for about 5 minutes, until smooth, adding more flour if necessary. Place in a clean bowl, cover with a dish towel, and set in a warm spot to rise for 30 minutes, or until the dough has doubled in size.
4. While the dough is rising, make the filling. Place the mushrooms in a small bowl and cover with boiling water. Steep for 30 minutes.
5. Dice the seitan. Finely chop the onion and garlic. Drain the mushrooms and slice into thin strips.
6. Heat the peanut oil in a sauté pan over high heat. Sauté the onions and mushrooms for 5 minutes, or until softened.
7. Add the garlic and five-spice powder and cook for another 2 minutes. Stir in the soy sauce. Add the sesame oil and reduce the heat to low. Cook for 5 minutes, or until the liquid evaporates. Remove from the heat.
8. Deflate the dough and divide into 16 equal pieces. Roll each piece into a ball, then flatten into a round ⅛ inch (3 mm) thick. Place about 2 tablespoons of the filling in the middle of each wrapper. Gather up the edges of each wrapper and twist to seal. Place each bun on a small square of parchment paper.
9. Place a steamer insert in a large pot and pour in water to reach just below the insert. Place the buns, on their parchment squares, on the steamer insert. Cover the pot and bring to a boil over high heat. Lower the heat so the water still boils gently. Steam until puffy and firm, 15 to 20 minutes, adding more boiling water if needed. Serve warm.

Tip

We love serving these dumplings with our Vietnamese Cucumber Salad (page 39) and some sriracha drizzled on top.

PARTY HITS

We love eggplant!

EGGPLANT KOFTA

MIDDLE EASTERN FINGER FOOD

PREPARATION TIME 35 minutes • COOKING TIME 25 minutes • MAKES 16 kofta

These savory Turkish eggplant patties can easily be prepared in advance in larger quantities for a party or gathering. Just fry them up at the start of the festivities.

- 2 tablespoons ground flaxseed
- 1 pound (500 g) eggplant (1 medium eggplant)
- 2 tablespoons salt
- 5 tablespoons olive oil
- 2 scallions
- 2 garlic cloves
- 1 tablespoon soy sauce
- 1⅓ cup (150 g) bread crumbs
- ¼ cup (60 g) plain soy yogurt
- 2 teaspoons Turkish red pepper flakes or other red pepper flakes

1. Mix the flaxseed with ¼ cup (60 ml) water. Set aside for 10 minutes.
2. Cube the eggplant and put it in a colander. Toss with the salt. Let drain for 10 minutes.
3. Rinse the eggplant and drain well. Dry with paper towels.
4. Heat 2 tablespoons of the oil in a large sauté pan over medium-high heat. Add the eggplant and sauté for about 5 minutes, until golden brown.
5. Add 3½ tablespoons water to the pan and cook the eggplant for an additional 5 minutes, until softened. Remove from the heat and set aside.
6. Slice the scallions and mince the garlic.
7. Combine the eggplant, flaxseed mixture, scallions, garlic, soy sauce, and bread crumbs in a large bowl. Mix well. Shape into 16 patties.
8. Heat the remaining 3 tablespoons oil in a large sauté pan over medium heat. Working in batches if necessary, fry the patties until crisp, for about 7 minutes on each side.
9. Top with the yogurt and red pepper flakes and serve.

Tip

These kofta pair well with our Flatbread (page 169) and a fresh salad. We also like rolling them up in tortillas for lunch on the go.

ANTIPASTO PIZZA BITES

PREPARATION TIME 30 minutes • COOKING TIME 30 minutes • MAKES 8 small pizzas

Pizza bites—need we say more?
Ours are topped with the best antipasti and are destined
to be a big hit with your guests.

- 1 eggplant
- 1 zucchini
- 1 onion
- 4 serrano chiles or jalapeños
- ¼ cup (60 ml) plus 1 tablespoon olive oil
- 1½ teaspoons salt
- Basic Pizza Dough (page 165)
- 4 to 5 tablespoons tomato paste
- 1½ tablespoons dried oregano
- 1 teaspoon agave syrup
- 3 garlic cloves
- 1¼ cups (150 g) shredded vegan cheese (such as cheddar)

1. Preheat the oven to 425°F (210°C). Line two baking sheets with parchment paper.
2. Thinly slice the eggplant, zucchini, and onion. Mince the chiles. Combine the eggplant, zucchini, onion, chiles, ¼ cup (60 ml) of the oil, and 1 teaspoon of the salt in a large bowl. Spread the mixture in an even layer on one of the prepared baking sheets and roast for 20 minutes, or until golden brown.
3. Remove from the oven. Transfer the vegetables to a plate and rinse the baking sheet to cool it. Line with another piece of parchment. Turn the oven up to 450°F (230°C).
4. Divide the dough into 8 pieces and roll out each piece to a round ½ inch (13 mm) thick.
5. To make the pizza sauce, combine the tomato paste, oregano, the remaining ½ teaspoon salt, the agave syrup, and the remaining 1 tablespoon oil in a small bowl.
6. Finely mince the garlic and mix it with the roasted vegetables.
7. Place the pizza dough rounds on the prepared baking sheets, spread with the sauce, and top with the roasted vegetables and vegan cheese. Bake for 8 minutes, or until the crust is golden. Cut into wedges and serve.

Tip

If you don't have time to roast the vegetables for the pizza topping, replace them with a selection of antipasti from your supermarket or local Italian deli.

Sooo
Yummy!

GINGER NORI CAKES

WITH SRIRACHA MAYONNAISE

PREPARATION TIME 20 minutes • COOKING TIME 10 minutes

CHILLING TIME 20 minutes • MAKES 10 cakes

We hope you try these toasty little cakes with a Japanese touch. The slightly sweet and salty flavor of the nori is a fun addition to a party buffet table. These also make a great sandwich filler.

- 3 tablespoons ground flaxseed
- Salt
- 1 pound (500 g) russet potatoes, peeled
- 1 large onion
- 2 garlic cloves
- 1 thumb-sized piece ginger
- ½ red jalapeño or other fresh red chile
- 1 scallion
- 2 sheets nori
- 4 tablespoons peanut oil
- 1 tablespoon soy sauce
- 1½ cups (250 g) drained cooked chickpeas
- 1 teaspoon ground coriander
- ⅓ cup (40 g) gluten-free bread crumbs
- Lettuce leaves or chopped lettuce, for serving
- ¼ cup (60 g) Sriracha Mayo (page 183)
- 1 tablespoon sesame seeds

1. Combine the flaxseed with ¼ cup plus 2 tablespoons (90 ml) water in a small bowl. Set aside for 10 minutes.
2. Bring a pot of salted water to boil. Cube the potatoes and cook for 10 minutes in the boiling water, until fork-tender. Drain and let cool slightly.
3. Finely chop the onion, garlic, ginger, and jalapeño. Thinly slice the scallion. Cut the nori into thin strips.
4. Heat 2 tablespoons of the oil in a sauté pan over medium heat. Add the onions, garlic, jalapeño, ginger, and nori. Sauté for 4 minutes, until softened. Add the soy sauce, stir, and remove from the heat. Transfer to a food processor.
5. Add the chickpeas, potatoes, coriander, and flaxseed. Pulse until coarsely chopped. Transfer to a bowl and refrigerate for 20 minutes.
6. Shape the mixture into 10 cakes. Coat the cakes with the bread crumbs.
7. Heat the remaining 2 tablespoons oil in a large sauté pan over medium-high heat. Working in batches if necessary, fry the cakes until crisp, for about 5 minutes on each side.
8. Arrange the lettuce on a serving platter. Place the cakes on top. Drizzle with the mayo and sprinkle with the sesame seeds.

SAVORY CORN WAFFLES

WITH PICO DE GALLO

PREPARATION TIME 10 minutes • COOKING TIME 20 minutes • MAKES 8 waffles

Dig out your waffle iron—it's time for something new! These hearty waffles are made with cornmeal to give them a touch of Mexican flavor.

- 2 cups (250 g) fine cornmeal
- 1½ teaspoons baking powder
- 1 tablespoon dried oregano
- 1 teaspoon salt
- 2 tablespoons olive oil
- 1¼ cups (300 ml) rice milk
- Pico de Gallo (page 181), for serving

1. Preheat the oven to 200°F (95°C). Preheat the waffle iron to medium-high.
2. Whisk together the cornmeal, baking powder, oregano, and salt in a large bowl. Whisk in 1½ tablespoons of the oil, the milk, and 1 cup (240 ml) water until smooth.
3. Brush the waffle iron with some of the remaining oil. Ladle batter into the waffle iron, close, and cook until golden brown and crisp, 7 to 8 minutes for each waffle. Put the waffle on a baking sheet and keep warm in the oven. Repeat until the batter is gone.
4. Serve hot with pico de gallo.

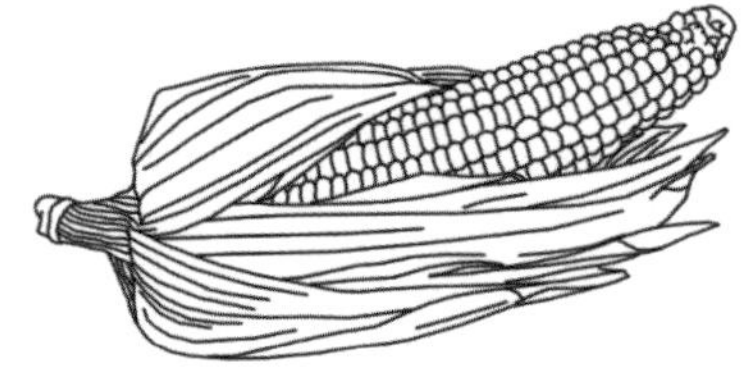

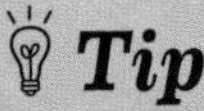

Tip

Pico de gallo isn't the only accompaniment for the waffles, of course. We love serving them with a hot bowl of vegan chili as well.

ROASTED SWEET POTATOES

ARGENTINIAN STYLE

PREPARATION TIME 5 minutes • BAKING TIME 45 minutes • SERVES 4

Fun fact: The sweet potato is only distantly related to the regular potato, and actually comes from the morning glory family. Crammed with essential nutrients and vitamins, it's very versatile and tastes especially good when roasted.

- 4 large sweet potatoes
- 4 tablespoons olive oil
- 2⅓ cups (400 g) cooked black beans, drained
- Chimichurri (page 181)
- 2 tablespoons chopped fresh cilantro
- 1 teaspoon sea salt

1. Preheat the oven to 350°F (180°C). Line a baking sheet with parchment paper.
2. Poke the sweet potatoes all over with a fork. Rub them with 2 tablespoons of the oil. Put them on the prepared baking sheet and place in the oven.
3. Mix the beans with the remaining 2 tablespoons oil. When the sweet potatoes have been roasting for 20 minutes, scatter the beans next to the potatoes and continue to roast for an additional 25 minutes, or until the potatoes are soft.
4. When the sweet potatoes are cooked through, halve them lengthwise. Fill with the beans and chimichurri, then top with the cilantro. Sprinkle with the salt and serve.

THAI TEMPURA

CRUNCHY VEGGIES

PREPARATION TIME 30 minutes • SERVES 4

Tempura is a classic Japanese dish. Instead of deep-frying the vegetables, we panfry them and give the tempura a touch of Southeast Asian flavors.

FOR THE DIPPING SAUCE

½ fresh red chile

¼ cup (60 ml) rice vinegar

FOR THE VEGETABLES

9 ounces (250 g) broccoli

9 ounces (250 g) cauliflower

1 carrot, peeled

1 cup (100 g) white button mushrooms

1 onion

⅓ cup (75 ml) peanut oil, for frying

Chopped cilantro, to serve

FOR THE BATTER

3 makrut lime leaves

1 cup (125 g) all-purpose flour

1 tablespoon cornstarch

1 teaspoon baking powder

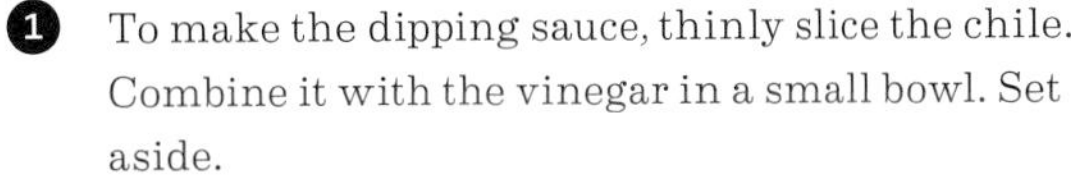

1. To make the dipping sauce, thinly slice the chile. Combine it with the vinegar in a small bowl. Set aside.

2. To prepare the vegetables, cut the broccoli and cauliflower into florets. Slice the carrot. Halve the mushrooms. Slice the onion into rings.

3. To make the batter, first thinly slice the lime leaves. Whisk together the flour, cornstarch, baking powder, lime leaves, and 1 cup (240 ml) cold water until smooth.

4. Heat the oil in a sauté pan over high heat. Working in batches, dip the vegetables into the batter, letting the excess drip off, then fry for about 4 minutes, until golden brown. Transfer to a paper towel–lined plate to drain. Top with cilantro and serve with the dipping sauce.

Tip

For a variation, try our beer tempura. Leave out the makrut lime leaves and replace the water with the same amount of very cold beer.

BAVARIAN SAMOSAS

PREPARATION TIME 35 minutes • MAKES 12 samosas

This recipe is the definition of fusion cuisine! Our Bavarian Samosas are filled with chewy sauerkraut, creamy potatoes, and sweet pineapple. They get an extra kick from Indian spices. We especially love the asafetida, also known as hing*—you can find this at most Indian grocery stores, so don't skip it!*

- 1 large onion
- 3½ ounces (100 g) russet potato (1 small), boiled and peeled
- ¼ cup (50 g) cubed peeled fresh pineapple
- 1⅓ cups (200 g) drained sauerkraut
- 1 teaspoon salt
- 4½ ounces (125 g) smoked tofu
- 2 garlic cloves
- 3 teaspoons curry powder
- 2 teaspoons asafetida
- ½ teaspoon ground coriander
- 2 tablespoons soy milk
- 24 spring roll wrappers
- 2 tablespoons peanut oil

1. Preheat the oven to 350°F (180°C). Line a baking sheet with parchment paper.
2. Slice the onion into thin rings. Cube the potato. Combine the onion, potato, and pineapple with the sauerkraut and salt in a medium bowl.
3. Blend the tofu, garlic, curry powder, asafetida, coriander, and milk until smooth in a small food processor. Add to the sauerkraut mixture and mix well.
4. Lay one of the spring roll wrappers on top of another. Spoon 2 tablespoons of the filling in the middle, brush the edge with a little water, and fold into a triangle. Repeat with the remaining wrappers and filling.
5. Brush the samosas with the oil and place on the prepared baking sheet.
6. Bake for 20 minutes, or until golden brown. Serve warm.

TACO LETTUCE WRAPS

WITH LENTIL-BULGUR CHILI

PREPARATION TIME 10 minutes • COOKING TIME 25 minutes • MAKES 16 tacos

Crunchy lettuce leaves filled with our lentil-bulgur chili are a light and tasty alternative to the crisp fried taco shell.

1 onion
3 garlic cloves
2 tablespoons olive oil
2 teaspoons dried oregano
1½ teaspoons ground cumin
1 tablespoon tomato paste
1 teaspoon agave syrup
1 cup (150 g) bulgur
⅔ cup (100 g) drained canned or thawed frozen corn kernels
1 cup (200 g) red lentils
1⅔ cups (400 ml) vegetable broth
Salt and freshly ground black pepper
1 teaspoon red pepper flakes
16 romaine lettuce leaves
4 limes, quartered

1. Dice the onion. Finely chop one of the garlic cloves.
2. Heat the oil in a medium saucepan over medium heat. Sauté the onion until translucent, about 4 minutes. Add the chopped garlic, oregano, and cumin and cook for another 3 minutes.
3. Add the tomato paste, agave syrup, the remaining garlic cloves, the bulgur, corn, and lentils. Cook for about 3 minutes, stirring frequently.
4. Add the broth and cover. Cook for 15 minutes, until the liquid has reduced.
5. Season to taste with salt, pepper, and the red pepper flakes. Serve on the lettuce leaves with the limes alongside.

Tip

Our Nacho Dip (page 181) goes perfectly with these lettuce wraps. We also love serving them with Pico de Gallo (page 181).

SWISS CHARD PIE

SICILIAN STYLE

PREPARATION TIME 30 minutes • RESTING TIME 30 minutes
BAKING TIME 20 minutes • MAKES one 8-inch (20 cm) pie

Swiss chard season lasts from spring to fall. Its delicate flavor pairs wonderfully with sweet raisins and balsamic vinegar in this savory Sicilian pie.

FOR THE PASTRY

- 2⅓ cups (300 g) spelt flour
- ⅓ cup (80 g) vegan butter
- 1 teaspoon coarse sea salt

FOR THE FILLING

- 2 garlic cloves
- 2 onions
- 2 tablespoons olive oil
- 3 teaspoons raisins
- 1 bunch Swiss chard
- 2 teaspoons blanched raw almonds
- 1 teaspoon red pepper flakes
- 1 tablespoon balsamic vinegar
- 2 tablespoons nutritional yeast

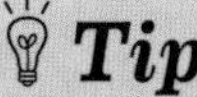

Tip

Fresh chard is the best chard, so use it soon after buying. Wrapped up in a damp dish towel, it will keep in the fridge for a couple of days.

1. To make the pastry, combine the flour, vegan butter, and salt in a food processor with ½ cup (120 ml) cold water. Pulse until smooth. Wrap the dough in plastic wrap and refrigerate for 30 minutes.
2. To make the filling, finely dice the garlic and onions. Heat the oil in a large sauté pan over medium heat. Cook the onions, garlic, and raisins for about 5 minutes, until softened.
3. Cut the chard crosswise into thin strips, including the stems. Coarsely chop the almonds. Add the chard, almonds, and red peppers flakes to the pan and cook for a minute or two. Add the vinegar and reduce the heat to low. Cook for 10 minutes, or until greens are tender.
4. Preheat the oven to 350°F (180°C).
5. Roll out three-quarters of the pastry to an 11-inch (28 cm) circle and place it on an 8-inch (20 cm) pie plate or tart pan, preferably with a removable bottom. Press it down across the bottom and up the sides.
6. Stir the nutritional yeast into the Swiss chard mixture. Spread it evenly over the pastry.
7. Roll out the remaining pastry to fit the top of the pie and place it on top. Pinch the edges together. Cut a few slits into the top of the pie.
8. Bake for 20 minutes, or until golden brown. Serve warm.

CHICKPEA TART

WITH SPINACH PESTO

PREPARATION TIME 15 minutes • RESTING TIME 30 minutes
BAKING TIME 20 minutes • MAKES One 11-inch (28 cm) tart

This tart is a variation of the flatbread socca, which is a popular street food in the south of France. You can also top this tart with avocado slices or a fresh salad.

- 2¼ cups (250 g) chickpea flour
- ¼ cup (60 ml) olive oil
- 2 garlic cloves, minced
- 1 teaspoon herbes de Provence
- Salt
- ⅓ cup (50 g) frozen peas
- ¼ cup plus 2 tablespoons (85 g) Spinach-Cashew Pesto (page 187)
- ½ bunch fresh chives, minced
- ½ lemon, thinly sliced

1. Whisk together the chickpea flour, 2 cups (480 ml) water, 3 tablespoons of the oil, the garlic, herbes de Provence, and 1 teaspoon salt in a large bowl until smooth. Set the batter aside for 30 minutes.

2. Preheat the oven to 350°F (180°C). Grease an 11-inch (28 cm) springform pan with the remaining oil. Fill a bowl with cold water and ice to make an ice bath.

3. Spread the batter evenly in the pan. Bake for 20 minutes, or until golden brown.

4. Meanwhile, bring a small pot of water to a boil and blanch the peas for 3 minutes, until defrosted and tender. Drain and transfer immediately to the ice bath to stop them from cooking. When the peas are cool, drain.

5. Remove the tart from the oven and spread evenly with the pesto. Top with the peas, chives, and lemon. Unmold and serve hot.

Tip

You can find chickpea flour at well-stocked grocery stores and vegetarian markets, as well as Indian grocery stores, where it is known as gram flour. If you have a high-speed blender, you can also make your own from dried chickpeas.

BREADS

easy &
delicious

BASIC PIZZA DOUGH

NEVER ORDER PIZZA AGAIN!

PREPARATION TIME 20 minutes • PROOFING TIME 1 hour • MAKES 4 pizzas

With this recipe, making pizza dough that tastes as good as your local pizzeria's is easy. Most of us don't have a wood-burning oven in our backyards, so a pizza stone for your oven is a great budget-friendly option.

- 2¼ teaspoons (1 packet) active dry yeast
- 4 cups (500 g) spelt flour, plus more for kneading
- 2 teaspoons salt
- Oil, for the bowl
- ¼ cup (35 g) cornmeal or ground semolina, for baking

1. Combine 1⅓ cups (320 ml) warm water with the yeast in a small bowl. Set aside until the yeast dissolves, about 10 minutes.
2. Combine the flour and salt in a large bowl. Add the yeast and stir until the dough comes together.
3. On a floured work surface, knead the dough until smooth, about 10 minutes.
4. Place the dough in a large oiled bowl and cover with a dish towel. Set aside until the dough has doubled in size, about 1 hour.
5. Divide the dough into quarters and roll them into even balls.
6. If you're baking the pizzas now, preheat the oven to 450°F (230°C). Line two baking sheets with parchment paper and sprinkle them with the cornmeal. Roll out each piece of dough to a round ½ inch (13 mm) thick and place on the prepared baking sheets. Top with your desired ingredients. Bake for 10 to 12 minutes, until the crust is lightly brown. Serve hot.

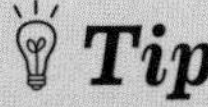

Tip

You don't need to bake all of the dough at once. If you have leftover dough, roll it into a ball and place it in a plastic bag. Refrigerate for up to 2 weeks or freeze it. When you thaw it, let it rise again for 20 minutes once it has reached room temperature.

GARLIC NAAN
WITH CILANTRO

PREPARATION TIME 20 minutes • PROOFING TIME 1 to 2 hours
COOKING TIME 25 minutes • MAKES 4 breads

India has such a wide selection of wonderful breads and flatbreads. From chapatis to parathas, there's a bread for every kind of dish. We love these stuffed naan flatbreads. You don't need a traditional tandoori oven to make them—a nonstick pan with a lid works very well.

FOR THE DOUGH

1 teaspoon (about ½ packet) active dry yeast

2 cups (250 g) spelt flour, plus more for kneading

1 teaspoon salt

2 tablespoons olive oil, plus more for the bowl

3 tablespoons plain soy yogurt, plus more for serving

2 teaspoons agave syrup

FOR THE FILLING

½ bunch fresh cilantro, plus more to serve

4 garlic cloves

Salt and fresh ground black pepper

1. To make the dough, stir 1½ cups plus 1 tablespoon (375 ml) warm water into the yeast in a small bowl. Set aside until the yeast dissolves, about 10 minutes.
2. Combine the flour and salt in a large bowl. Add the yeast, oil, yogurt, and agave syrup, stirring until it forms a shaggy dough.
3. On a floured work surface, knead the dough until smooth, about 5 minutes.
4. Place the dough in a large oiled bowl and cover with a dish towel. Set aside for 1 hour, or until the dough has doubled in size.
5. To make the filling, finely chop the cilantro and garlic. Season with salt and pepper.
6. Divide the risen dough into quarters. Roll out each quarter to a round ¼ inch (6 mm) thick.
7. Spread the filling down the middle of each dough round. Fold the dough in half over the filling, then roll out again to ovals ¼ inch (6 mm) thick.
8. Sprinkle the naans with water. Place a dry pan over high heat. Place a naan in the pan, cover, and cook for 3 minutes on each side, or until golden brown. Repeat with all the naans.
9. Top with cilantro and serve warm with yogurt.

Tip

You can try making these naan filled with mashed potatoes and spiced with garam masala. We also love eating naan with curry or dal.

FLATBREAD

JUST LIKE IN MOROCCO

PREPARATION TIME 35 minutes • PROOFING TIME 1½ to 2 hours
BAKING TIME 30 minutes • MAKES 1 flatbread

There are hardly any Moroccan dishes that don't come served with bread. We like this simple flatbread, which pairs well with lots of different meals.

- 1 teaspoon (about ½ packet) active dry yeast
- 1 teaspoon maple syrup
- 1 tablespoon olive oil, plus more for the bowl
- 2 cups (250 g) spelt flour, plus more for kneading
- 1 teaspoon salt

1. Whisk the yeast in a small bowl with the maple syrup, oil, and ½ cup (120 ml) warm water. Set aside until the yeast dissolves, about 10 minutes.
2. Combine the flour and salt in a large bowl. Add the yeast mixture and stir until a shaggy dough forms.
3. On a floured work surface, knead the dough until smooth, about 10 minutes.
4. Place the dough in an oiled bowl and cover with a dish towel. Set aside to rise for 1 hour, or until the dough has doubled in size.
5. Punch down the dough, then shape to a round loaf. Cover and let proof for another 30 minutes.
6. While the dough rises, preheat the oven to 425°F (200°C). Line a baking sheet with parchment paper.
7. Place the loaf on the prepared baking sheet. Using a sharp knife or razor, cut an X in the top of the loaf.
8. Bake for 20 minutes. Rotate the baking sheet and bake for another 10 minutes, until golden brown.
9. Remove the sheet from the oven and place on a wire rack. Let the loaf cool completely before slicing and serving.

Tip

To make the bottom of the bread even crisper, scatter a bit of ground semolina on the parchment paper before transferring the loaf to the baking sheet.

SAVORY SCONES
WITH RAMPS & SUN-DRIED TOMATOES

PREPARATION TIME 15 minutes • RESTING TIME 15 minutes
BAKING TIME 20 minutes • MAKES about 10 scones

Originally from Scotland, these little pastries are traditionally served with jam and cream at afternoon tea. They've also become popular as savory pastries. We love them flavored with freshly picked ramps or scallions and salty-sweet sun-dried tomatoes.

- 1⅔ cups (200 g) spelt flour, plus more for rolling
- 1½ teaspoons baking powder
- 1 teaspoon salt
- 2 tablespoons vegan butter
- 1 tablespoon dried oregano
- 3 tablespoons nutritional yeast
- ½ cup (120 ml) oat milk
- Small bunch ramps, trimmed and chopped
- 5 oil-packed sun-dried tomatoes, drained and chopped

1. Whisk together the flour, baking powder, and salt in a large bowl. Add the vegan butter, working it into the flour with your fingers until the dough is crumbly.
2. Add the oregano, nutritional yeast, milk, ramps, and tomatoes. Knead just until the dough comes together. Try not to overwork.
3. Wrap the dough in plastic wrap and refrigerate for 15 minutes.
4. Meanwhile, preheat the oven to 350°F (180°C). Line the baking sheet with parchment paper.
5. On a floured work surface, roll out the dough to 1¼ inches (3 cm) thick. Cut into rounds using a biscuit cutter or wine glass.
6. Place the scones on the prepared baking sheet and bake for 20 minutes, or until golden brown.

Tip

You can vary the dried herbs and flavorings you use in these savory scones. Try them with chopped olives, rosemary, spinach, or basil.

DINNER ROLLS

AN AMERICAN CLASSIC

PREPARATION TIME 20 minutes • PROOFING TIME 1 hour
BAKING TIME 15 minutes • MAKES 6 rolls

These buttery-soft warm rolls are just the thing to mop up the last drops of sauce on your plate.

- 1 teaspoon (about ½ packet) active dry yeast
- 2 cups (250 g) spelt flour, plus more for kneading
- 1 teaspoon salt
- 1 teaspoon granulated sugar
- 1 tablespoon (20 g) vegan butter, melted
- Oil, for greasing the bowl and baking dish
- 2 tablespoons soy milk

1. Whisk ½ cup (120 ml) warm water into the yeast in a small bowl. Set aside until the yeast dissolves, about 10 minutes.
2. Combine the flour, salt, and sugar in a large bowl. Add the yeast mixture, followed by the vegan butter, and stir. When a shaggy dough forms, knead on a floured work surface until smooth, about 5 minutes.
3. Place the dough in an oiled bowl, cover with a dish towel, and set aside for 1 hour, or until the dough has doubled in size.
4. Meanwhile, preheat the oven to 400°F (200°C). Lightly grease a baking pan.
5. Punch down the dough and divide it into 6 equal portions. Roll into balls and place in the baking pan.
6. Brush the rolls with the milk. Bake for 15 minutes, or until lightly browned. Serve warm.

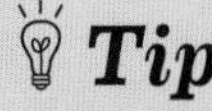

For extra flavor, add 2 finely minced garlic cloves to the vegan butter before mixing it into the dough. Garlic rolls are great with our Roasted Squash Soup (page 95).

BAGELS

PREPARATION TIME 35 minutes • PROOFING TIME 1 hour
BAKING TIME 20 minutes • MAKES 10 bagels

Bagels aren't an American invention. In fact, they originated in Poland and came to the United States with Jewish immigrants, later becoming a permanent fixture of the American breakfast table.

- 2¼ teaspoons (1 packet) active dry yeast
- 4 cups (500 g) spelt flour, plus more for kneading
- 2 teaspoons salt
- 2 tablespoons granulated sugar
- Sesame seeds, poppy seeds, and/or caraway seeds, optional

1. Whisk 1¼ cups (300 ml) warm water into the yeast in a small bowl. Set aside until the yeast dissolves, about 10 minutes.
2. Combine the flour and salt in a large bowl. Add the yeast mixture and stir until a shaggy dough forms.
3. On a floured work surface, knead the dough until smooth, about 5 minutes.
4. Place the dough in a large bowl and cover with a dish towel. Set aside for 1 hour, or until the dough has doubled in size.
5. Bring 2 quarts (2 L) water to a boil and add the sugar. Preheat the oven to 425°F (210°C). Line the baking sheet with parchment paper.
6. Divide the dough into 10 equal portions. Shape the dough into balls, then poke a hole in the middle and smooth into rings.
7. Working in batches, place the rings in the boiling water and simmer for 3 minutes. Remove with a skimmer and place the rings on the baking sheet.
8. Sprinkle with seeds, if using. Bake for 20 minutes, or until golden brown.

Tip

We like to cut these bagels in half while they're still warm and eat them with vegan butter and a sprinkle of minced chives. So good! They also make a great base for our spreads (page 191).

FOCACCIA

EASY AS PIE

PREPARATION TIME 45 minutes • PROOFING TIME 1 hour
BAKING TIME 30 minutes • SERVES 4

Fresh focaccia is an integral part of breakfast in northwestern Italy. The bread is similar to pizza, but thicker. Here we make a classic version with rosemary and sun-dried tomatoes.

- 1 tablespoon (about 1¼ packets) active dry yeast
- ¼ cup (60 ml) olive oil, plus 2 tablespoons, and more for the bowl
- 2 tablespoons coarse sea salt
- 4 cups (500 g) spelt flour, plus more for kneading
- 1 tablespoon cornmeal
- 5 oil-packed sun-dried tomatoes, drained and chopped
- Leaves from 2 sprigs fresh rosemary

1. Whisk 1⅓ cups (320 ml) warm water into the yeast in a small bowl. Set aside until the yeast dissolves, about 10 minutes.
2. Stir ¼ cup (60 ml) plus 1 tablespoon of the oil and 1 tablespoon of the salt into the yeast. Combine the yeast mixture with the flour in a large bowl and stir with a wooden spoon.
3. On a floured work surface, knead the dough for about 10 minutes, until smooth and elastic.
4. Place the dough in an oiled bowl and cover with a dish towel. Set aside for 1 hour, or until the dough has doubled in size.
5. Preheat the oven to 400°F (200°C). Line a baking sheet with parchment paper and sprinkle with the cornmeal.
6. Punch down the dough, then spread out on the prepared baking sheet. Drizzle with the remaining 1 tablespoon oil.
7. Sprinkle the chopped tomatoes and rosemary evenly over the dough and press gently into the surface. Sprinkle with the remaining salt.
8. Bake for 30 minutes, or until slightly golden brown and cooked through.

Tip

Instead of rosemary and tomatoes, try topping the focaccia with cured olives, pickled peppers, or just freshly ground black pepper.

DIPS, PESTO & MORE

SUPER DIPS

BALANCED

Delectable dips for every occasion! Our versatile recipes aren't just for chips, pretzel sticks, or crackers—they're also great accompaniments for many of the recipes in this book. These delicious dips will last for up to a week in covered containers in the refrigerator.

EACH MAKES About 1 cup (240 g)

CHIMICHURRI

PREPARATION TIME 10 minutes

½ bunch fresh cilantro • 1 bunch fresh parsley
1 garlic clove • ¼ cup (60 ml) white wine vinegar
½ teaspoon dried oregano, plus more if needed
⅓ cup (75 ml) olive oil
Salt and freshly ground black pepper

1. Coarsely chop the cilantro, parsley, and garlic.
2. Place the cilantro, parsley, garlic, vinegar, oregano, and 3 tablespoons water in a food processor or blender. Pulse to combine. While the motor is running, stream in the oil and process until smooth. Season to taste with salt, pepper, and more oregano, if you like.

GLUTEN-FREE • SUGAR-FREE • SOY-FREE

LIME HUMMUS

PREPARATION TIME 5 minutes
ROASTING TIME 20 minutes

4 cubanelle peppers
One 15-ounce (425 g) can chickpeas, drained
2 tablespoons tahini • 2 garlic cloves • Juice of 1 lime
½ teaspoon ground cumin
½ teaspoon ground coriander • ½ teaspoon salt

1. Preheat the oven to 350°F (180°C).
2. Roast the peppers on a sheet pan for 20 minutes, until softened and charred.
3. Place the roasted peppers, chickpeas, tahini, garlic, lime juice, cumin, coriander, and salt in a food processor and blend until smooth.

GLUTEN-FREE • SUGAR-FREE • SOY-FREE

NACHO DIP

PREPARATION TIME 10 minutes
COOKING TIME 10 minutes

Salt • 3 medium russet potatoes, peeled • 1 carrot, peeled
½ red bell pepper, stemmed and seeded
⅔ cup (100 g) raw cashews • 1 garlic clove
⅓ cup (20 g) nutritional yeast
2 teaspoons olive oil • 2 teaspoons onion powder
⅓ cup plus 2 tablespoons (110 ml) oat milk

1. Bring a large pot of salted water to boil. Dice the potatoes, carrot, and bell pepper. Add to the boiling water and cook until just tender, about 10 minutes. Drain and let cool.
2. Place the potatoes, carrot, bell pepper, cashews, garlic, nutritional yeast, oil, onion powder, and milk in a food processor and blend until smooth. Return to the pot and bring to a brief boil. Season with 1 teaspoon salt and then serve.

GLUTEN-FREE • SOY-FREE

PICO DE GALLO

PREPARATION TIME 10 minutes

5 medium tomatoes • ½ medium onion
½ bunch fresh cilantro • 1 garlic clove • 1 fresh red chile
Juice of 1 lime • Salt

1. Dice the tomatoes. Finely chop the onion, cilantro, and garlic. Slice the chile into thin rings. Combine the tomatoes, onion, cilantro, garlic, chile, and lime juice in a bowl. Season to taste with salt.

GLUTEN-FREE • SUGAR-FREE • SOY-FREE

FOUR MAYOS

PREPARATION TIME 5 minutes • MAKES About 1 cup (250 g)

We've spent countless hours in grocery aisles looking for an eggless mayonnaise. What a waste of time, when it's so easy to make at home. All of these mayos will last for up to a week in a covered container in the refrigerator.

BASIC MAYO

¼ cup (60 ml) soy milk

1 tablespoon apple cider vinegar

½ teaspoon mustard

½ teaspoon salt

½ cup (120 ml) canola oil

FOR AÏOLI

2 garlic cloves, minced

FOR WASABI MAYO

2 teaspoons wasabi paste

FOR SRIRACHA MAYO

1½ tablespoons sriracha

1. Put the milk, vinegar, mustard, salt, and ¼ cup (60 ml) of the oil in a blender. Turn on the machine and blend until smooth.
2. With the motor running, slowly stream in the remaining ¼ cup (60 ml) oil. Blend until smooth.
3. Add the flavoring of your choice, if any, and continue to blend until smooth.

PRESERVED LEMONS

MOROCCAN STYLE

PREPARATION TIME 20 minutes • PRESERVING TIME 4 weeks • MAKE 4 lemons

Preserved lemons are an integral part of Moroccan cooking. With their unusual and aromatic flavor, they give couscous, vegetables, and stews a certain je ne sais quoi.

8 lemons

1 fresh red chile

2 garlic cloves, peeled

¾ cup (200 g) sea salt

10 black peppercorns

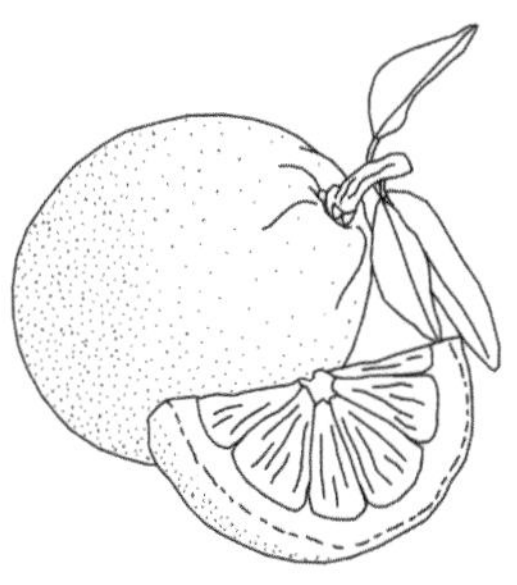

1. Juice 2 of the lemons and set the juice aside.
2. Wash the remaining 4 lemons well with hot water. Leaving them attached at one end, cut the lemons into quarters.
3. Halve the chile lengthwise. Crush the garlic.
4. Pack the cuts in the lemons with salt, then place the lemons in a sterilized 1-quart (1 L) canning jar with the chile, garlic, and peppercorns.
5. Fill the jar with any remaining salt and top with the lemon juice and enough water to cover the lemons completely.
6. Seal the jar and place it in a cool dark spot for 4 weeks.
7. When ready to use, rinse the lemons, discard the flesh, and slice the peel into thin slices.

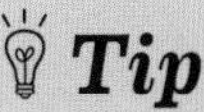

Tip

Preserved lemons are great in our Chickpea Sumac Salad (page 45), tabbouleh, and North African stews, and even as a topping for pasta.

HOMEMADE

TANGY PESTOS

BALANCED

Pack your homemade pestos in small canning jars and top with a little olive oil to help preserve their freshness. They'll keep in the fridge for a couple of weeks, but we don't think you'll wait that long to finish them.

EACH MAKES About 1 cup (230 g)

SPINACH-CASHEW PESTO

PREPARATION TIME 10 minutes

⅓ cup (75 ml) plus 1 tablespoon olive oil
9 ounces (250 g) baby spinach • 2 garlic cloves
2 tablespoons raw cashews • 1 tablespoon raw almonds
1 tablespoon nutritional yeast • 1 teaspoon salt

1. Heat 1 tablespoon of the oil in a large sauté pan over medium-high heat. Add the spinach and sauté for 2 minutes, until it has all wilted. Let cool.
2. Transfer the spinach to a blender or food processor. Add the garlic, cashews, almonds, nutritional yeast, salt, and the remaining ⅓ cup (75 ml) oil and blend until smooth.

GLUTEN-FREE • SUGAR-FREE • SOY-FREE

ROASTED TOMATO PESTO

PREPARATION TIME 5 minutes
ROASTING TIME 20 minutes

14 ounces (400 g) fresh tomatoes
⅓ cup (75 ml) plus 1 tablespoon olive oil
3 oil-packed sun-dried tomatoes • ¼ cup (40 g) raw cashews
3 tablespoons nutritional yeast
3 tablespoons chopped fresh parsley
1 tablespoon chopped fresh basil • 1 teaspoon salt

1. Preheat the oven to 400°F (200°C). Line a baking sheet with parchment paper.
2. Halve the fresh tomatoes. Place them cut side down on the prepared baking sheet. Brush with 1 tablespoon of the oil and roast for 20 minutes, until softened and charred. Let cool.
3. Transfer the roasted tomatoes to a blender or food processor. Add the remaining ⅓ cup (75 ml) oil, the sun-dried tomatoes, cashews, nutritional yeast, parsley, basil, and salt and blend until smooth.

GLUTEN-FREE • SUGAR-FREE • SOY-FREE

ARUGULA-PUMPKIN SEED PESTO

PREPARATION TIME 10 minutes

¼ cup plus 2 tablespoons (50 g) shelled raw pumpkin seeds
6 loosely packed cups (120 g) arugula
¼ cup plus 2 tablespoons (90 ml) olive oil
1 tablespoon nutritional yeast • Juice of ½ lemon
1 teaspoon salt • ¼ teaspoon freshly ground black pepper

1. Toast the pumpkin seeds in a dry pan over medium-high heat for 4 minutes, until golden brown, stirring constantly. Let cool.
2. Transfer the seeds to a blender or food processor. Add the arugula, oil, nutritional yeast, lemon juice, salt, and pepper and blend until smooth.

GLUTEN-FREE • SUGAR-FREE • SOY-FREE

LEEK-WALNUT PESTO

PREPARATION TIME 15 minutes

½ leek, white and green parts, trimmed and rinsed
⅓ cup (75 ml) plus 1 tablespoon olive oil
¼ cup (25 g) walnuts • 1 garlic clove
1 tablespoon nutritional yeast
½ tablespoon grated lemon zest • 1 teaspoon salt

1. Thinly slice the leek.
2. Pour 1 tablespoon of the oil into a sauté pan over medium-high heat. Add the leek and cook until soft, about 5 minutes. Let cool.
3. Transfer the leek to a blender or food processor. Add the remaining ⅓ cup (75 ml) oil, walnuts, garlic, nutritional yeast, lemon zest, and salt and blend until smooth.

GLUTEN-FREE • SUGAR-FREE • SOY-FREE

VIETNAMESE PICKLES

LIGHT

PREPARATION TIME 15 minutes • MAKES 4 cups (620 g)

These pickled vegetables are the star of our Bánh Mì Deluxe (page 37). They're quick to put together and are just as good as an afternoon snack or as a side at a barbecue.

- 3 carrots, peeled
- 1 daikon (about 1 pound/450 g), peeled
- 1 red onion
- ½ teaspoon salt
- 3 tablespoons granulated sugar
- ½ cup (120 ml) rice vinegar or white wine vinegar

1. Slice the carrots and daikon into strips 2 inches (5 cm) long and ¼ inch (6 mm) thick. Slice the onion into rings. Place the vegetables in a large bowl.
2. Add the salt and 2 teaspoons of the sugar. Massage for about 3 minutes.
3. Rinse the vegetables under cold running water. Drain well.
4. Combine the remaining 2 tablespoons plus 1 teaspoon sugar, the vinegar, and ⅓ cup (75 ml) warm water in a small bowl. Stir until the sugar dissolves.
5. Place the vegetables in a quart-sized (1 L) sterilized canning jar and cover with the pickling liquid.
6. Serve immediately or cover and refrigerate for up to 3 weeks.

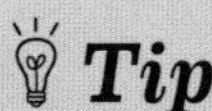

Tip

You can adapt this recipe to use up most of the vegetables hanging out in your fridge.

OUR FAVORITE SPREADS

BALANCED

Nowadays it's easy to find a wide array of interesting and tasty vegan spreads at the grocery store. But homemade spreads taste fresher and don't require additional ingredients for shelf stability. These super spreads will last for up to a week in covered containers in the refrigerator.

EACH MAKES About 1 cup (230 g)

ROASTED EGGPLANT SPREAD

PREPARATION TIME 15 minutes
ROASTING TIME 20 minutes

9 ounces (250 g) eggplant • Salt
3 tablespoons olive oil
¾ cup (100 g) raw shelled sunflower seeds
2 teaspoons dried oregano • 1 teaspoon ground paprika
½ teaspoon freshly ground black pepper

1. Preheat the oven to 400°F (200°C). Line a baking sheet with parchment paper.
2. Cube the eggplant, mix with salt, and drain in a colander for 10 minutes.
3. Remove excess liquid with a paper towel.
4. Mix the eggplant with the oil and spread in an even layer on the prepared baking sheet. Roast for 20 minutes, until softened and charred. Let cool.
5. Transfer the roasted eggplant to a food processor. Add the sunflower seeds, oregano, paprika, 2 teaspoons salt, and pepper and blend until smooth.

GLUTEN-FREE • SUGAR-FREE • SOY-FREE

TOMATO MACADAMIA RICOTTA

PREPARATION TIME 5 minutes

¾ cup (100 g) raw macadamia nuts
4 ounces (120 g) silken tofu
7 oil-packed sun-dried tomatoes, drained
2 tablespoons soy milk • 1 teaspoon salt
½ teaspoon freshly ground black pepper

Combine the macadamia nuts, tofu, tomatoes, milk, salt, and pepper in a food processor and process until smooth.

GLUTEN-FREE • SUGAR-FREE

PROVENÇAL SPREAD

PREPARATION TIME 5 minutes

1⅓ cups (250 g) drained cooked kidney beans
1 garlic clove • ½ teaspoon dried rosemary
½ teaspoon dried oregano • ½ teaspoon salt
½ teaspoon freshly ground black pepper

Combine the beans, garlic, rosemary, oregano, salt, and pepper in a food processor and process until smooth.

GLUTEN-FREE • SUGAR-FREE • SOY-FREE

OYSTER MUSHROOM TAPENADE

PREPARATION TIME 15 minutes

7 ounces (200 g) oyster mushrooms
3½ ounces (100 g) white button mushrooms
2 garlic cloves • 2 tablespoons olive oil
1 tablespoon fresh thyme leaves • 3 tablespoons white wine
¼ cup (45 g) mixed pitted olives
1 tablespoon drained capers
1 tablespoon chopped fresh parsley
Salt and freshly ground black pepper

1. Finely chop the mushrooms and garlic.
2. Heat the oil in a large sauté pan over medium heat. Add the mushrooms, garlic, and thyme and cook for about 4 minutes, until softened.
3. Add the wine and simmer for 5 minutes, until the liquid has reduced.
4. Transfer the mushroom mixture to a food processor. Add the olives, capers, and parsley and process until smooth. Season to taste with salt and pepper.

GLUTEN-FREE • SUGAR-FREE • SOY-FREE

AGED CASHEW CHEESE

HEARTY AND NUTTY

PREPARATION TIME 10 minutes • SOAKING TIME 4 hours or overnight
FERMENTING TIME 24 hours • AGING TIME 7 to 10 days
MAKES One 10½-ounce (300 g) cheese

Who would have thought that you could use nuts to make such a luscious vegan cheese? And it's so easy to boot! Once you've made your own cheese, we're pretty sure it will become a staple.

- 1⅓ cups (200 g) raw cashews
- ½ cup (120 ml) fermented grain beverage, such as rejuvelac
- 1½ teaspoons salt
- 1 teaspoon ground paprika

1. Place the cashews in a large bowl and cover with water. Cover and set aside to soak at room temperature for at least 4 hours or overnight.
2. Drain and rinse the cashews. Transfer them to a food processor. Add the rejuvelac and salt and blend until smooth.
3. Pour the mixture into a bowl, cover, and set aside in a warm spot to ferment for 24 hours.
4. Spoon the mixture into a cheesecloth and squeeze out the excess liquid.
5. Form the mass into a round loaf. Sprinkle all over with the paprika and loosely wrap in wax paper. Refrigerate for 7 to 10 days to ripen.

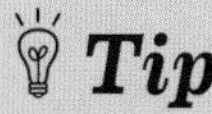

Tip

Before ripening, you can also sprinkle the cheese with multicolored peppercorns, caraway seeds, aniseed, coriander seeds, or a mix of dried herbs.

SAUCES & SPICE MIXES

Easy and economical to make at home, these sauces and spices give our recipes the perfect final touch.

EACH MAKES About 1 cup (230 g)

HARISSA

PREPARATION TIME 35 minutes

3½ ounces (100 g) dried whole chiles, such as guajillo
½ teaspoon ground coriander • ½ teaspoon ground cumin
3 garlic cloves • 1 tablespoon tomato paste
1 teaspoon agave syrup • Juice of ½ lemon
¼ cup (60 ml) olive oil

1. Soak the chiles in hot water for 30 minutes. Drain, discarding the soaking water. Remove and discard the stems from the chiles. Tear the chiles into pieces and place in a food processor.
2. Toast the coriander and cumin in a dry pan over medium-high heat for 4 minutes, stirring constantly, until toasted. Let cool, then add to the chiles.
3. Add the garlic, tomato paste, agave syrup, and lemon juice to the chiles. Blend, slowly streaming in the oil, until the harissa is smooth.

GLUTEN-FREE • SOY-FREE

DUKKAH

PREPARATION TIME 15 minutes

½ cup (75 g) mixed raw nuts
2 tablespoons sesame seeds • 2 tablespoons coriander seed
1 tablespoon cumin seeds • ½ teaspoon salt
½ teaspoon freshly ground black pepper

1. Toast the nuts and the sesame, coriander, and cumin seeds in a dry pan over medium-high heat for 4 minutes, stirring constantly, until golden. Let cool, then transfer to a food processor.
2. Add the salt and pepper and pulse to combine. Store in an airtight container for up to 2 weeks.

GLUTEN-FREE • SUGAR-FREE • SOY-FREE

FAKE FISH SAUCE

PREPARATION TIME 1 hour

4 nori sheets • 3 garlic cloves
1 teaspoon freshly ground black pepper
⅓ cup plus 1 tablespoon (95 ml) soy sauce

1. Cut the nori into thin strips, Combine with 2⅓ cups (560 ml) water in a small pot. Simmer for 20 minutes.
2. Add the garlic, pepper, and soy sauce and cook for 30 minutes over medium heat, until reduced by half.
3. Strain through a fine-mesh sieve into a glass jar or bottle. Let cool, then cap. Store in the refrigerator for up to 1 week.

GLUTEN-FREE • SUGAR-FREE

YUM YUM SAUCE

PREPARATION TIME 10 minutes

2 teaspoons sesame seeds • 1 garlic clove
1 scallion • 3 tablespoons soy sauce
1 tablespoon dark (toasted) sesame oil
½ teaspoon rice vinegar
2 teaspoons red pepper flakes • ½ teaspoon agave syrup

1. Toast the sesame seeds in a dry pan over medium-high heat for 4 minutes, stirring constantly, until golden brown. Let cool.
2. Finely mince the garlic. Thinly slice the scallion.
3. Combine the sesame seeds, garlic, scallion, soy sauce, oil, vinegar, red pepper flakes, and agave syrup in a small bowl or a jar. Store in the refrigerator for up to 1 week.

GLUTEN-FREE • SUGAR-FREE • SOY-FREE

Ball
MASON

SAVORY TOFU FETA

GREEK ANTIPASTO

PREPARATION TIME 10 minutes • RESTING TIME 3 days • MAKES 1 cup (155 g)

This vegan substitute for herbed feta is super easy to make and so yummy. Don't discard the valuable herb oil after you've eaten up the cheese and vegetables—it makes a great base for a lovely salad dressing.

- 7 ounces (200 g) smoked tofu
- 4 oil-packed sun-dried tomatoes
- 4 green olives, pitted
- 4 black olives, pitted
- 1 fresh red chile
- 5 sprigs fresh oregano
- Handful of fresh basil leaves
- 2 teaspoons salt
- Olive oil as needed

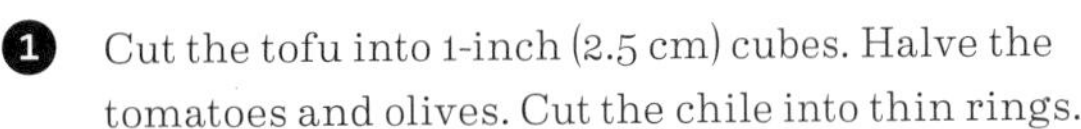

1. Cut the tofu into 1-inch (2.5 cm) cubes. Halve the tomatoes and olives. Cut the chile into thin rings.
2. Place the tofu, tomatoes, olives, chile, oregano, and basil in a 1-quart (1 L) sterilized glass jar. Sprinkle with the salt and fill the jar with oil to cover everything. Cover with the jar lid.
3. Let sit at room temperature for at least 3 days.

SWEET STUFF

MOCHA CUPCAKES

WITH CASHEW-KAHLÚA FROSTING

PREPARATION TIME 20 minutes • SOAKING TIME 2 hours • BAKING TIME 20 minutes
CHILLING TIME 70 minutes • MAKES 12 cupcakes

These decadent cupcakes are a dreamy mix of chocolate and coffee. They're topped with a wonderful cashew cream and Kahlúa frosting.

FOR THE FROSTING

1⅓ cups (200 g) raw cashews

⅓ cup (75 ml) Kahlúa or other coffee liqueur

¼ cup (60 ml) almond milk

¼ cup (40 g) cocoa butter chips, melted and cooled

3 tablespoons powdered sugar

A few chocolate-covered coffee beans

FOR THE CUPCAKES

⅓ cup (75 ml) canola oil, plus more for the muffin pan

2 cups (240 g) spelt flour

¾ cup (140 g) brown or muscovado sugar

¼ cup (25 g) unsweetened cocoa powder

1 teaspoon baking powder

1 teaspoon baking soda

1 teaspoon vanilla extract

¼ cup (60 g) unsweetened applesauce

¼ cup plus 2 tablespoons (90 ml) espresso (a double shot)

½ cup plus 2 tablespoons (150 ml) almond milk

1. To start the frosting, place the cashews in a large bowl and cover with water. Cover and set aside to soak for at least 2 hours.

2. Preheat the oven to 350°F (180°C). Lightly grease a muffin pan or line the cups with paper liners.

3. To make the cupcakes, combine the flour, sugar, cocoa, baking powder, and baking soda in a large bowl. Whisk together the oil, vanilla, applesauce, espresso, and milk in a medium bowl. Pour the liquid mixture into the dry mixture and stir until smooth.

4. Spoon 2 tablespoons of the batter into each cup of the muffin pan. Bake for 20 minutes, or until golden and springy to the touch.

5. Remove from the oven and place the pan on a wire rack to cool completely.

6. While the cupcakes cool, make the frosting. Drain the cashews, rinse, and drain again. Place the cashews, Kahlúa, milk, cocoa butter, and powdered sugar in a food processor. Pulse until smooth.

7. Transfer the frosting to a bowl and chill for 10 minutes, until it firms slightly.

8. Fit a piping bag with a decorative tip and transfer the frosting to the bag. Top the cooled cupcakes with the frosting.

9. Coarsely chop the coffee beans and sprinkle on top of the frosting. Chill for at least 1 hour before serving.

REFRESHING HORCHATA

WITH RICE & ALMONDS

PREPARATION TIME 30 minutes • STEEPING TIME 12 hours or overnight
CHILLING TIME 12 hours • MAKES 1 quart (1 L)

Horchata is a creamy summer drink beloved in both Mexico and Spain, though the preparations differ. Mexican horchata is made with rice and almonds, while Spanish horchata is made with soaked and ground tiger nuts. Both are vegan! This drink can be made ahead and refrigerated for up to 3 days.

1 cup plus 2 tablespoons (180 g) skin-on raw almonds

$2\frac{1}{2}$ tablespoons rice flour

1 cinnamon stick

3 tablespoons agave syrup

1. Bring a pot of water to a boil. Blanch the almonds for 2 minutes, then drain. When the almonds have cooled, squeeze the nutmeats out of the skins.
2. Toast the almonds in a dry pan over medium heat for 10 minutes, stirring frequently, until golden brown.
3. Combine the almonds, rice flour, cinnamon stick, and $3\frac{1}{4}$ cups (780 ml) hot water in a bowl. Cover and steep at least 12 hours or overnight at room temperature.
4. Working in batches if necessary, pour the mixture into a blender. Add 1 cup (240 ml) cold water and the agave syrup. Blend until smooth.
5. Strain the horchata through cheesecloth into a bottle or pitcher. Chill for at least 12 hours.
6. Serve over ice.

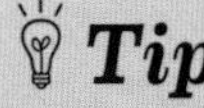

Tip

In the mood for a creamy Mexican cocktail? Add 1 tablespoon plus 1 teaspoon good-quality tequila to a glass of horchata. Alternatively, you can add dark rum and a shot of pineapple juice.

BERRY CHEESECAKE

WITHOUT TURNING ON THE OVEN

PREPARATION TIME 25 minutes • SOAKING TIME 1 hour
CHILLING TIME 3 hours • MAKES One 6-inch (15 cm) cake

Consider this recipe a little introduction to the world of raw food. We think this cheesecake is just as delightful as its traditional cousin—it's an indulgence that just happens to be healthy.

FOR THE CHEESECAKE FILLING

2 cups (300 g) raw cashews
2 teaspoons grated lemon zest
Juice of 1 lemon
Seeds scraped from 1 vanilla bean
3 tablespoons agave syrup
2 tablespoons almond milk
2 tablespoons coconut oil
Handful of fresh berries, plus more to serve

FOR THE CRUST

1½ tablespoons coconut oil
1 cup plus 1 tablespoon (170 g) raw almonds
¼ cup (60 g) pitted dates

1. To start the filling, place the cashews in a bowl and cover with water. Cover and soak for 1 hour.
2. To make the crust, melt the coconut oil. Combine the oil, almonds, and dates in a food processor and pulse until smooth.
3. Line a 6-inch (15 cm) springform pan with plastic wrap. Press the crust evenly into the bottom of the pan. Set aside.
4. To make the filling, drain, rinse, and drain the cashews again. Transfer the cashews to a food processor or blender. Add the lemon zest, lemon juice, vanilla bean seeds, agave syrup, milk, and oil and blend until smooth. Add more agave syrup if you want it sweeter, and/or more milk if the mixture is too thick.
5. Spread two-thirds of the cheesecake filling over the crust.
6. Add the berries to the remaining filling in the food processor and purée until smooth. Spread this evenly over the plain filling layer. Garnish with additional berries. Refrigerate for at least 3 hours before unmolding and serving.

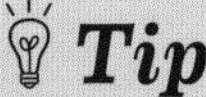

If you place the cheesecake in the freezer instead, you will have an exquisite frozen berry cheesecake for hot summer days!

NICE CREAM SANDWICHES

GLORIOUSLY DECADENT

PREPARATION TIME 30 minutes • BAKING TIME 10 minutes
CHILLING AND FREEZING TIME 1 hour • MAKES 4 sandwiches

Who can resist creamy coconut mocha "nice cream" sandwiched between two soft chocolate cookies? Not us!

FOR THE COOKIES

1 tablespoon ground flaxseed

1½ tablespoons cocoa butter chips

⅔ cup (80 g) spelt flour

⅓ cup (60 g) muscovado or brown sugar

3 tablespoons unsweetened cocoa powder

1 teaspoon baking powder

3 tablespoons oat milk

½ teaspoon apple cider vinegar

Pinch of salt

FOR THE NICE CREAM

Half of a 13.5-ounce (400 ml) can coconut cream

Half of a 13.5-ounce (400 ml) can full-fat coconut milk

½ cup (80 g) muscovado or brown sugar

3 tablespoons espresso

½ teaspoon vanilla paste or vanilla extract

1. Preheat oven to 350°F (180°C). Line a baking sheet with parchment paper.
2. Stir 2 tablespoons water into the flaxseed in a medium bowl. Set aside for 10 minutes.
3. Melt the cocoa butter and add it to the flaxseed. Add the flour, sugar, cocoa, baking powder, milk, vinegar, and salt and whisk or stir until smooth.
4. Shape the dough into 8 rounds, about 2 inches (5 cm) apart, on the prepared baking sheet. Bake for 10 minutes, or until the edges begin to crisp. Let the cookies cool on the pan on a wire rack, then place in the freezer for 1 hour.
5. While the cookies are freezing, make the nice cream. Combine the coconut cream, coconut milk, sugar, espresso, and vanilla in a saucepan over medium heat and cook, stirring constantly, just until the sugar has dissolved.
6. Remove from the heat. Let the nice cream base cool completely, then churn in an ice cream machine.
7. Sandwich 1 large scoop of nice cream between 2 frozen cookies, pressing them firmly together. Repeat with the remaining nice cream and cookies. If not serving immediately, put them back on the baking sheet and keep them in the freezer.
8. The nice cream sandwiches will keep for several weeks in an airtight container in the freezer. Remove from the freezer about 20 minutes before serving.

TAPIOCA PUDDING

WITH COCONUT MILK & MANGO

PREPARATION TIME 40 minutes • CHILLING TIME 1 hour • SERVES 4

This pudding makes a deliciously light summer dessert or lovely treat when you're hit with a sudden craving for something sweet. The rum gives it a refined touch for special occasions.

¼ cup plus 2 tablespoons (55 g) tapioca pearls

2½ cups (600 ml) full-fat coconut milk

¼ cup (60 ml) agave syrup

3 tablespoons rum

1 mango, peeled, pitted, and cubed

2 tablespoons unsweetened dried coconut chips

1. Bring 1 quart (1 L) water to a boil in a saucepan. Add the tapioca pearls and cook, covered, for 15 minutes. Remove from the heat and let sit for 15 additional minutes, uncovered, then drain.

2. Stir together the coconut milk, agave syrup, and rum in a saucepan over medium heat. When the mixture is hot, add the tapioca. Bring to a boil and cook for 5 minutes, until it forms a pudding-like consistency.

3. Remove the pot from the heat and divide the mixture among four dessert bowls. Let cool completely, then refrigerate for at least 1 hour.

4. Before serving, top the pudding with the mango and sprinkle with the coconut chips.

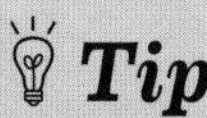

Tip

This pudding can be adapted with any topping you like such as berries, kiwis, honeydew melon, passionfruit, or toasted nuts. Make it your own!

MINI BROWNIE TART

MOIST & CHOCOLATEY

PREPARATION TIME 15 minutes • BAKING TIME 40 minutes • MAKES one 6-inch (15 cm) tart

Calling all chocoholics! Our incredibly moist brownie tart, swirled with a rich peanut-almond cream, is incredibly chocolatey—and entirely flourless.

- 1 tablespoon ground flaxseed
- 1½ tablespoons coconut oil
- 1 cup plus 2 tablespoons (200 g) cooked and drained black beans
- ⅓ cup (25 g) unsweetened cocoa powder
- 3 tablespoons muscovado or brown sugar
- 1 teaspoon baking powder
- Pinch of salt
- 1¾ ounces (50 g) vegan chocolate
- 2 tablespoons natural peanut butter
- 1 tablespoon almond butter

GLUTEN FREE

1. Preheat the oven to 350°F (180°C). Line a 6-inch (15 cm) springform pan with parchment paper.
2. Stir 2 tablespoons water into the flaxseed in a small bowl. Cover and set aside for 10 minutes.
3. Melt the coconut oil. Transfer to a food processor. Add the beans, cocoa, sugar, baking powder, and salt and process until smooth.
4. Coarsely chop the chocolate and fold into the batter. Spread the batter evenly into the prepared pan.
5. Mix together the peanut and almond butters and drizzle over the batter. Use a fork or wooden skewer to swirl the nut butters in a marbleized pattern across the batter.
6. Bake for 40 minutes, or until the batter is just set to the touch. Cool completely on a wire rack before unmolding and cutting.

NOM
NOM
NOM

PEANUT TRUFFLES

CHOCOLATE & PEANUTS GALORE!

PREPARATION TIME 15 minutes • FREEZING TIME 1 hour • MAKES 20 truffles

These heavenly bites—filled with a delectable peanut filling—remind us of Snickers bars.

- 1 ⅔ cups (170 g) rolled oats
- ½ cup (80 g) raw almonds
- ½ cup (80 g) unsalted roasted peanuts
- ¾ cup (200 g) natural peanut butter
- 3 tablespoons maple syrup
- 3½ ounces (100 g) bittersweet vegan chocolate

1. Pulse the oats, almonds, and peanuts in a food processor until finely ground.
2. Transfer to a medium bowl. Add the peanut butter and maple syrup and mix well. Roll into small balls and place on a baking sheet. Cover and place in the freezer for 1 hour.
3. Melt the chocolate in a heatproof bowl over boiling water or in the microwave. Dip the frozen balls into the chocolate, then set them on a wire rack to dry.
4. Store in an airtight container in the freezer until ready to serve.

APPLE-PEAR COFFEE CAKE

FRUITY! SPICY! DELICIOUS!

PREPARATION TIME 20 minutes • BAKING TIME 1 hour • SERVES 4

Our Apple-Pear Coffee Cake is a tempting twist on the classic recipe with a soft, moist cake topped with richly spiced streusel. It's the perfect treat with your afternoon tea or coffee.

FOR THE CAKE

2 tablespoons ground flaxseed

¾ cup plus 1 tablespoon (100 g) spelt flour

¼ cup (50 g) unrefined cane sugar

½ teaspoon ground cinnamon

¼ teaspoon baking soda

1 teaspoon vanilla extract

2½ tablespoons plain soy yogurt

2 tablespoons unsweetened applesauce

2 tablespoons sunflower oil

½ tablespoon apple cider vinegar

1 apple, peeled

1 pear, peeled

FOR THE STREUSEL TOPPING

1 tablespoon vegan butter

1½ tablespoons all-purpose flour

2 teaspoons granulated sugar

1 teaspoon ground cinnamon

1. To make the cake, stir ¼ cup (60 ml) water into the flaxseed in a medium bowl. Let sit, covered, for 10 minutes.
2. Preheat the oven to 350°F (180°C). Line a 6-inch (15 cm) springform pan with parchment paper.
3. Whisk together the flour, sugar, cinnamon, and baking powder in a large bowl. Whisk the vanilla, yogurt, applesauce, oil, and vinegar into the flaxseed. Pour the wet ingredients into the dry ingredients and stir until smooth. Spread the batter into the prepared pan.
4. Cut the fruit into thin slices. Top the batter with the sliced fruit.
5. To make the streusel, combine the vegan butter, flour, sugar, and cinnamon in a bowl. Mix with your fingers until it clumps together. Distribute evenly over the cake.
6. Bake for 1 hour, or until golden brown.
7. Cool for at least 15 minutes on a wire rack before unmolding and serving.

BANANA POPSICLES

PREPARATION TIME 20 minutes • FREEZING TIME 5 hours • MAKES 4 popsicles

Super simple and unbelievably good, banana popsicles are the perfect, refreshing dessert for hot summer days.

2 bananas

1 tablespoon raw almonds

1 tablespoon dried coconut chips

1¾ ounces (50 g) vegan chocolate

1. Peel the bananas and halve them horizontally. Spear each half on a popsicle stick or straw and lay flat on a baking sheet. Freeze for at least 5 hours.
2. Finely chop the almonds and coconut. Toast them together for 10 minutes in a dry pan over medium heat, stirring constantly, until golden brown.
3. Melt the chocolate in a shallow heatproof bowl over boiling water or in the microwave.
4. Remove the bananas from the freezer and dip in the melted chocolate, then roll in the almonds and coconut.
5. Place on a wire rack to let the chocolate set briefly, then serve.

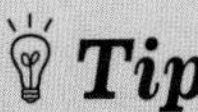

Tip

We also love dipping these popsicles in chopped pistachios, cornflakes, or finely ground dried coconut.

ACKNOWLEDGMENTS

We'd like to thank our loyal blog readers, who were the first ones to make our cookbook possible.

To Nessa, who graced the pages of this book with her wonderful illustrations and always had an open ear for us.

To our parents, who supported us unequivocally and were always by our sides with advice and helping hands.

To NeunZehn Verlag—Kristina, Walter, Uli, and the rest of the team—for trusting in us!

To all vegans and animal rights activists for your hard work.

Additionally, our gratitude goes to:

Miri, Evelyn, Anja, Maxi, Sandra and Jens, Isa and Manu, Simon, the graphic design department of mission <one>, Pascal, Max, Nobby, Fla, and Café Naschkatze in Neu-Ulm and Café Pano in Ulm for their help, interest, and support.

Last but not least, to you, dear reader!

INDEX

Page numbers in *italics* indicate photographs.

MORE BY NADINE HORN AND JÖRG MAYER

ALSO AVAILABLE FROM THE EXPERIMENT

VBQ—THE ULTIMATE VEGAN BARBECUE COOKBOOK: OVER 80 RECIPES—SEARED, SKEWERED, SMOKING HOT!

BBQ, make way for *VBQ*: smoky, succulent, and completely plant-based barbecued fare. Nadine Horn and Jörg Mayer have transformed the art of grilling into a veggie lover's feast—complete with Grilled Bok Choy, Peppered Tofu Steak, and everything in between.

"The good-for-the-planet call to arms continues its crescendo [with] *VBQ—The Ultimate Vegan Barbecue Cookbook.*"

—*The New York Times Book Review*

224 pages
$19.95 US | $25.95 CAN
Paperback: 978-1-61519-456-8
Ebook: 978-1-61519-457-5

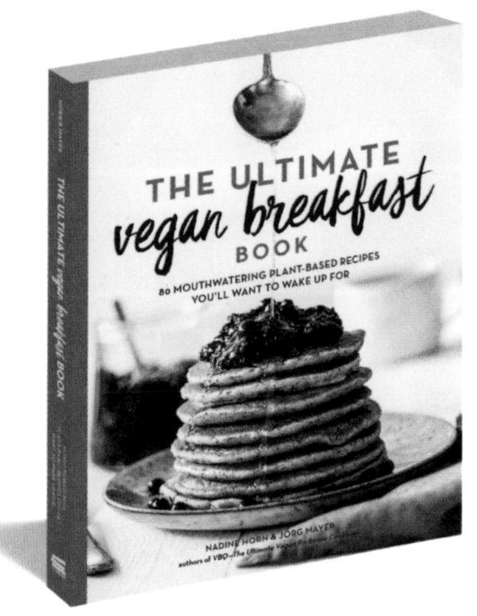

THE ULTIMATE VEGAN BREAKFAST BOOK: 80 MOUTHWATERING PLANT-BASED RECIPES YOU'LL WANT TO WAKE UP FOR

Plant-ify your mornings with *The Ultimate Vegan Breakfast Book.* Vegans will have a new reason to say "good morning" thanks to these satisfying, nutritious, and flavorful recipes including Breakfast Burritos, Tempeh Bacon, Power Waffles, and more.

"Horn and Mayer make vegan breakfast fun and satisfying to cook, eat, and share."—*Publishers Weekly*

208 pages
$19.95 US | $25.95 CAN
Paperback: 978-1-61519-488-9
Ebook: 978-1-61519-515-2